MILTON'S
'PARADISE LOST'

Gul. Faithorne ad Virum
Delin. et sculpsit.

Joannis Miltoni Effigies Ætat: 62.
1670.

A Portrait of Milton at the age of 62, by Faithorne (from Milton's *History of Britain*, 1670)

MILTON'S
'PARADISE LOST'

by

B. A. Wright

METHUEN & CO LTD

11 NEW FETTER LANE

LONDON EC4

First published 1962
Reprinted 1968
1.2
SBN 416 64800 9

First published as a University Paperback 1968
1.1
SBN 416 29680 7

*Printed offset in Great Britain
by The Camelot Press
Southampton*

*Distributed in the U.S.A. by
Barnes & Noble Inc.*

CONTENTS

PREFACE   *page* 9

1 THE MAN AND THE POET   13

2 THE MORAL IN THE FABLE   41

3 DICTION   62

4 THE FUNCTION OF THE   85
   EPIC SIMILE

5 SIMILES FROM VOYAGES   107
   OF DISCOVERY

6 GOD AND SATAN   118

7 i) ANGELS IN REVOLT   128
   ii) SATAN'S RETURN TO HELL   137

8 THE CREATION   147

9 PARADISE   154

10 THE FALL   166

11 AFTER THE FALL   179

12 THE LAST TWO BOOKS   190

   INDEX   207

TO PHYLL

PREFACE

Since the first war Milton has indeed 'fall'n on evil days, and evil tongues' in his own country. Young men and women go up to the universities to read Honours English without having read a line of him, for their teachers have told them that they need not bother with a poet of exploded reputation. *Paradise Lost* accordingly is not nowadays widely read or highly regarded. This situation has of course been brought about in special circumstances and by certain leading figures in the literary scene of our time; but the revulsion from *Paradise Lost* could not have happened without certain weaknesses and false trends in the previous, traditional appraisal of the poem, and it is these that must be seen and corrected if the balance is to be restored. First among these critical errors is that Milton the poet is not distinguished from Milton the man, and Milton the man is not distinguished from the ogre originally created by his religious and political enemies, and revived by Dr. Johnson a century later. I try to remove this stumbling block in my first chapter. I then deal with those aspects of the poem itself that to my mind have been misunderstood and misconstrued. First it is thought and said that *Paradise Lost* is 'a monument to dead ideas', yet they are ideas that had dominated Europe for over a thousand years and were still very much alive in the seventeenth century; and for the sensitive reader they still live in the action of the poem. One of my purposes is to show how the ideas are embodied in and borne out by the story, and I set them forth in chapter 2 solely with a view to this. Next it is thought that the language of the poem, not being the common English of its time, is now dead; this is mere ignorance, but un-refuted ignorance. We shall see that Milton speaks 'the tongue that Shakespeare spake'. In the first of the chapters on the epic similes I demonstrate their true function in portraying the scenes and characters of the poem; in the second I show that much of their material, far from being remote or merely literary, is taken from the contemporary world and from some of the most important events in then recent history. In the second half of the book I follow the course of the poem, beginning with the scene in Heaven in Book III, going on to the war in Heaven and to Satan's return to Hell after the Fall of man, then to the Creation of the world and, lastly, to the central story of Adam and Eve. In this second half I am above all concerned to reveal the power and skill of Milton's narrative art. Swimming against the tide of present opinion I do not expect to get anywhere, but tides turn.

The book is meant for the common reader and lover of poetry. There are accordingly very few footnotes; for if I may judge by myself the common reader does not like being distracted by these 'marginal stuffings', to use Milton's phrase, which he will not look up but cannot forbear looking at. Any essential references are given in the body of the text. All quotations from *Paradise Lost* are from my Everyman (revised) edition of *Milton's Poems*, 1959, corrected at places.

I wish to thank the following friends, who read the manuscript in whole or in part, for the time and trouble so generously given, and for their valuable criticisms and suggestions: Helen Gardner, the late A. W. Gomme, H. D. F. Kitto, J. J. Lawlor, and J. B. Leishman. Above all I am indebted to F. T. Prince who, besides many parti-cular criticisms, suggested a major addition that has improved the scope and balance of the book. Lastly, I have to thank K. R. Brooks for undertaking the laborious task of reading the page proofs. Needless to say, none of these friends is to be held responsible for my errors of fact, eccentricities of judgment or other short-comings.

B. A. W.

Chapter 1

THE MAN AND THE POET

I shall deal only with those aspects of *Paradise Lost* on which, to my sense, the common view is mistaken; even so there is plenty and to spare. Some general misconceptions need to be cleared up before coming to the examination of the poem itself: they concern the relation of the man to the poet and the relation of the poet's ideas to his poem. I deal with them in that order in the first two chapters.

Critics and readers of poetry are fond of arguing from the man to the poet, seeking to interpret the poetry by the medium of biography. The practice assumes that the poet in action is identical with the man engaged in his other activities; to put it in an old-fashioned way, that there is no such thing as poetic inspiration. It assumes that what happens in the normal everyday world can explain what happens in a poem; that if an incident in a poem corresponds to an incident in the poet's life, still better if a parallel can be drawn between the action of a poem and the tenor of the poet's life, we are thereby enabled to understand and interpret the poetry. It may even be claimed that what happens in the poem could not be understood without the knowledge of what happened in real life. Conversely this kind of critic assumes that what happens in the poem can be brought in as biographical evidence, can enlighten us on what happened in the poet's ordinary life. The distinction between the actual and the imaginary having been thus obliterated, it follows that circular arguments from biography to poetry and back, in which fact and fiction vouch for each other, can be indulged in without restraint. The effect of this bioliterary criticism, as it may be called, is to substitute biography for poetry and then confound them. It is popular because biography is easier to follow than the action of a poem.

It is true that a poet's experiences as a man among men will supply him with part or the whole of the subject-matter of his poetry; but when such experience has been converted into poetry it becomes a different thing in a unique world of its own. Poets themselves have testified to this fact, and none more emphatically than those of our own time. T. S. Eliot has said that, 'The mind of the poet . . . may partly or exclusively operate upon the experience of the poet himself; but, the more perfect the artist, the more completely separate in him will be the man who suffers and the mind which creates; the more perfectly will the mind digest and transmute the passions which are its material.' And W. H. Auden speaks exactly to our point when he says, that 'knowledge of an artist's life, temperament and opinions is unimportant to an understanding of his art.' The truth is that what we need to know of this autobiographical matter in a poem is there only as poetry.

It is also true that with a poet of a past age knowledge of his life and times may put us in the way of understanding his poetry more easily. Elucidation of unfamiliar conventions of thought and feeling, of references to historical figures and events, and even biographical facts, may be helpful in so far as these are matter of the poetry; just as a gloss on obsolete words, or on words that have changed their meaning, is helpful. This is just a question of enlightening a reader's ignorance, of proffering the knowledge instead of letting him gather it from the poem: it saves time and trouble. But these are the raw materials of a poem, and what a reader should be concerned with is not the raw materials but what the poet has made of them in the poem as it stands; he should be concerned not with the prosaic but the poetic facts, and the one should never be mistaken for the other. Too many are only happy and confident in their reading of poetry if they can substitute prosaic for poetic facts, as though they can find no sure footing in the domain of poetry itself and prefer mounting a stepping-stone to peer over the garden-wall.

Even though we knew all there was to know about a poem's sources, this by itself would not enable us to understand and enjoy it as poetry. And if we knew all there was to know about the man, this by itself would not enable us to understand the poet. But how much less than all we do know! This brings us to a slightly different aspect of the question – the incomplete and ambiguous nature of biographical evidence as an instrument of criticism, compared with the exact and definitive nature of the purely literary evidence of the text of a poem. Biography is not the exact science those who use it for literary criticism would seem to suppose. We know little enough about living men we are intimately acquainted with – indeed it is notorious that we do not even know ourselves: we know much less about men long dead and buried, however massive the documentation. The biographer's material moreover is indeterminate and immeasurable; we can never be sure that we have it all, or all that is pertinent. On the other hand we can usually know that we have all the words of a poem, and that they are final as well as complete. The critic whose appeal is to the text of a poem may misinterpret it, but all the evidence is there to check him by; given an agreed text we know what we are talking about. The bioliterary critic has first to create the image of the man he argues from; the literary critic has only to examine and argue from what has already been – *pace* the 'creative' literary critic – definitively created, and the only image he has to do with is that which may have been expressed within the poem. Finally, the image of

[15]

the man from which the bioliterary critic argues may be not only shadowy and uncertain, but may be demonstrably false on the biographical evidence itself. Once such a false composite image has been accepted by the common reader it is almost impossible to do away with it, because of the confusion of biography and poetry that is inherent in the whole process: if his attention is drawn to the contradictory biographical evidence he refers you to the image of the man he has been taught to find in the poetry. He has you coming and going.

The methods and effects of bioliterary criticism are most clearly exemplified in the history of the criticism of Milton's poetry; none has been so bedevilled by it. There are several reasons for this. One is that he is among the more auto-biographical of poets, in the sense that his poetry expresses not only a strong personality and mind but that he not infrequently alludes to himself and his circumstances. Yet even at these latter places he speaks as a poet within the poem, and we are quite out if we begin to think of Mr. John Milton on his other occasions. Take the prologue to Book III of *Paradise Lost*, where he invokes the light of God and is so led on to speak of his own blindness:

> So thick a drop serene has quencht thir Orbs,
> Or dim suffusion veild. Yet not the more
> Cease I to wander where the Muses haunt
> Clear Spring, or shadie Grove, or Sunnie Hill,
> Smit with the love of sacred song; but chief
> Thee *Sion* and the flowrie Brooks beneath
> That wash thy hallowd feet, and warbling flow,
> Nightly I visit: nor somtimes forget
> Those other two equald with me in Fate,
> So were I equald with them in renown,
> Blind *Thamyris* and blind *Mæonides*,
> And *Tiresias* and *Phineus* Prophets old.
> Then feed on thoughts, that voluntarie move

Harmonious numbers; as the wakeful Bird
Sings darkling, and in shadiest Covert hid
Tunes her nocturnal Note. Thus with the Year
Seasons return, but not to me returns
Day, or the sweet approach of Ev'n or Morn,
Or sight of vernal bloom, or Summers Rose,
Or flocks, or herds, or human face divine;
But cloud in stead, and ever-during dark
Surrounds me, from the cheerful ways of men
Cut off, and for the Book of knowledge fair
Presented with a Universal blanc
Of Natures works to mee expung'd and ras'd,
And wisdom at one entrance quite shut out.
So much the rather thou Celestial Light
Shine inward, and the mind through all her powers
Irradiate, there plant eyes, all mist from thence
Purge and disperse, that I may see and tell
Of things invisible to mortal sight.

[*P.L.*, iii. 25–55

The personal references in this beautifully argued movement, as Tillyard pointed out, serve to effect a main transition in the poetic action. This is the poet within his poem,
in the moment of inspiration, in the act of creation, 'with
his garland and singing robes about him'. It is not the blind
Mr. Milton, citizen of London, who could be seen any
day by passers-by, as described by Jonathan Richardson:
'I have heard many years since that he Us'd to Sit in a Grey
Coarse Cloath Coat at the Door of his House, near *Bun-hill*
Fields without *Moor-gate*, in Warm Sunny Weather to Enjoy
the Fresh Air, . . . and very Lately I had the Good Fortune
to have another Picture of him from an Ancient Clergy-man
in *Dorsetshire*, Dr. *Wright*; He found him in a Small House,
he thinks but One Room on a Floor; in That, up One pair of
Stairs, which was hung with a Rusty Green, he found *John
Milton*, Sitting in an Elbow Chair, Black Cloaths, and Neat
enough, Pale, but not Cadaverous, his Hands and Fingers

[17]

Gouty, and with Chalk Stones, among Other Discourse He expressed himself to This Purpose; that were he Free from the Pain This gave him, his Blindness would be Tolerable.' It will be admitted that these glimpses of the blind Milton in his habit as he lived, precious as they are for their own purposes, would make a disenchanting commentary on the prologue to Book III; yet this is just the sort of thing that passes for poetic commentary on *Paradise Lost*.

If one should distinguish between the poet in his 'singing robes' and the man in 'a Grey Coarse Cloath Coat' in an autobiographical passage, what is one to say of such bio-literary criticism of dramatic and narrative poetry? This has been the procedure of almost every critic and commentator of *Samson Agonistes*, which Milton himself calls 'A Dramatic Poem'. How many have not been taught to read this dramatic poem as autobiography? Verity expresses the attitude unambiguously: 'No one can read the play without perceiving that it has something more than an artistic value. For those who are familiar with the facts of Milton's life it serves as a record of his deepest feelings at the most tragic point of his career. It is not only that there was a strong parallel in personal experience between the poet and his hero – that each was blind, that each had been unhappy in marriage, that each passes his closing years in circumstances of isolation and disappointment, in a world which had gone against him, repelling his efforts to make it better and saner. But the parallel held good of the broad political and religious conditions of their respective times.' And so finally he calls it 'this drama of autobiography'. In similar vein Grierson calls it 'a dramatic vindication of his own life, and of his action and that of those he supported in the great historical crisis through which he had lived. . . . Many critics have noted the more obvious resemblances between Samson and Milton himself. He too had wedded a wife from among the Philistines and she had betrayed his fondest hopes. He too, as

[18]

Masson was the first to point out, had driven from the field a boasting Harapha in the person of Salmasius. And now he too was "fallen on evil days":

> Eyeless in *Gaza*, at the mill, with slaves,

left to unjust tribunals, under change of times. . . . He is thinking of himself as identified with "the Good Old Cause" which has gone under.'

All this is a good example of the circular arguments indulged in by the bioliterary critics. The poem is drawn on for the biographical 'facts' and these 'facts' are then used to interpret the poem as autobiographical drama; Milton's situation and experiences are presented in terms of Samson's and then it is said, Look how like Samson Milton is! The one hard fact on which this identification of the poet with his hero depends is that both were blind; all the rest are baseless conjectures, some of them positively contradicted by the testimony of those who knew Milton. There is no warrant for assimilating Milton's experience of married life, or his reflections on that experience, with Samson's; for one thing Milton forgave Mary Powell and took her back. And as for Verity's 'each had been unhappy in marriage', it is hard to see why Milton took Mary back unless on the contrary he was unhappy without her, or why he married twice more; his second and third marriages, on the evidence, were happy. Again, when Verity states that Milton in his last years was isolated and disappointed, his only warrant is the words used by the poet to depict Samson's predicament; the evidence of his intimates in these years is that Milton was surrounded by devoted friends, visited 'more than he desired' as a remarkable and famous man, and within the limits of human capacity content. Sir Herbert Grierson's picture, in *Milton and Wordsworth*, of Milton after the Restoration as a frustrated, embittered, disillusioned old man, a prophet turned pessimist, is a figment of his own imagination.

[19]

But even though the biography extracted from *Samson Agonistes* were sounder than it is it would still be bad criticism to use it as a principal means of interpretation. For where does it lead us? To thinking of Milton in London instead of Samson in Gaza, of Mary Powell instead of Dalilah, of Salmasius instead of Harapha, of Roundheads and Puritans instead of Danites, and of Cavaliers instead of Philistines. And having persuaded us to this undramatic way of reading, the critics with one accord exclaim on Milton's want of dramatic ability. The way to read *Samson Agonistes* is, I submit, as a dramatic poem on Samson. In so reading it we shall of course, as in reading any of Milton's poetry, be made aware of his ideas and convictions and outlook on life; Samson allows him to concentrate his experience and express his idea of the heroic. No poet, not even Shakespeare, can do other than write out of his own fund of experience and thought; in Shakespeare's case luckily we know next to nothing of the man and are free to attend to the dramatic poetry.

Just as *Samson Agonistes* has been ruined as drama by bioliterary criticism so has *Paradise Lost* been ruined as narrative poetry, especially by the replacement of Adam by John Milton and of Eve by Mary Powell. There is the great and moving scene in Book X when Eve goes on her knees to win Adam's forgiveness, which leads to their reconciliation to each other and to God:

> with Tears that ceas'd not flowing
> And tresses all disorderd, . . .
> Forsake me not thus, *Adam*, witness Heav'n
> What love sincere and reverence in my heart
> I bear thee, . . .   [*P.L.*, x. 910–16

At this turning point in the story we do not wish to be referred to Edward Phillips's account of the return of Mary Powell to her husband, 'making Submission and begging Pardon on her Knees before him', or to be told, as Verity tells us, 'Probably Milton's reconciliation with his wife was present to his thoughts.' I appeal to poets that this is most improbable; that this memory was not and could not be 'present' to the poet's thoughts when he was creating a universal scene, not recreating an actual occasion. Nor should it be present to *our* thoughts in reading the poem, for if it is we are not reading the poem. To substitute Mary Powell for Eve is an impious fraud.

Even the poetry of Wordsworth, who took himself as 'the main region' of his song, cannot be understood by concentrating on his biography. It was generally supposed, and still is, that the unearthing of the Annette Vallon affair gave us a better insight into his poetry and in particular revealed for the first time that he had a passionate nature. An anonymous writer in *The Times Literary Supplement* once declared that knowledge of 'the existence of Wordsworth's illegitimate daughter is necessary to an understanding of his poetry'. He grossly deceived himself. Anyone incapable of feeling and responding to the passion of Wordsworth's love poetry before hearing of his illegitimate daughter will be incapable of feeling and responding to it afterwards, for he will be susceptible to scandal rather than to poetry.

Knowledge about the man and his life then is likely to be a snare and a delusion in interpreting his poetry; and the more we know the greater the danger. Unfortunately we know more about John Milton than about any previous English poet. But the damage does not end there in Milton's case; for the bioliterary critics have got the biographical facts all wrong, the facts having been from the outset distorted by political and religious prejudice. Since there is little hope of bioliterary critics refraining from their practices the most one can do is to correct their facts for them. I shall therefore present the authentic portrait of the man so that they may have a chance, in their own way, of getting a glimpse of the poet.

[21]

To begin with we know what Milton looked like at intervals in his life, from portraits at the age of 10, as a young man, in his middle years, and at the age of 62, three years after the publication of *Paradise Lost*. Anyone who looks at the latter portrait, reproduced as a frontispiece to this volume, and then believes that Milton's character was as it is usually presented, will, as the Duke of Wellington said on another occasion of mistaken identity, believe anything. The many passages in his prose writings, telling of the events and circumstances, motives and aims of his life, make up a substantial autobiography; and if one thinks Milton an inveterate liar, as some do, there are no less than six contemporary Lives by others to attest the truth of his own account. Three of these – Aubrey, his nephew Edward Phillips, whom he brought up, and an anonymous biographer – knew Milton personally; these are our authentic sources. Phillips's Life appeared in his edition of Milton's *State Papers*, 1694; Aubrey's notes were not printed until 1813, and the Anonymous Life not until 1902. Of the others Anthony Wood used Aubrey's notes and the Anonymous Life, which had been sent him by Aubrey for his Life in *Fasti Oxonienses*; this was published in 1691 and so became the first Life of Milton to appear. John Toland's Life (1698) relied on Edward Phillips's. The last of the six, Jonathan Richardson's, appeared as a preface to his *Explanatory Notes and Remarks on 'Paradise Lost'* in 1734; he certainly knew the Lives by Wood and Toland, and there is some internal evidence that he also knew of Aubrey's Notes and Edward Phillips's Life; but the most important point is that he was 9 years old when Milton died and was able to draw on a living tradition for a number of new anecdotes as well as for his impression of Milton's character and personality; his testimony therefore comes after the first three in value. So that we have three first-hand biographies, and three others in support of them. Yet the traditional idea of Milton does not agree with this authentic evidence: it directly contradicts it in some material points, and distorts it in others. Compared with the original portrait it is a caricature. And this traditional idea has established itself so firmly that Helen Darbishire's edition of the *Early Lives* in 1932, which made them generally available for the first time, has had little perceptible effect on it.

Certainly this traditional idea of Milton goes back to his own lifetime, but it was originally due not to those who knew him but to those who only knew of him as a name or public figure. It represented the idea of what a notorious rebel against Church and State, a defender of regicides and servant of Cromwell, would necessarily be like. This bugbear picture of the man continued to prevail in the public mind after his death; although Milton was admired by the judicious few as the poet of *Paradise Lost*, he was more generally remembered as the author of various heresies, of some scandalous pamphlets on divorce, and of *Eikonoklastes* and *Pro Populo Anglicano Defensio*, apologies for king-killing and republican usurpation which had been burnt by the common hangman in 1660. So strong was the detestation of Milton on these grounds that it affected judgement on him as a poet. William Winstanley in his *Lives of the most famous English Poets*, published in 1687, says: 'John Milton was one, whose natural parts might deservedly give him a place amongst the principal of our English Poets, having written two Heroick Poems and a Tragedy; namely *Paradise Lost, Paradise Regain'd* and *Samson Agonistes*; but his fame is gone out like a Candle in a snuff, and his Memory will always Stink, which might have lived in honourable repute, had he not been a notorious Trayter; and most impiously and villanously bely'd that blessed Martyr, King Charles the First.' Winstanley was wrong about the extinction of Milton's fame, as Dryden could have foretold, but he was right about the stink and its persistence. Even Addison, as late as 1694, in his *Account of the Greatest English Poets*, concludes with these lines on Milton's prose writings:

> Oh! had the poet ne'er profan'd his pen,
> To varnish o'er the guilt of faithless men,
> His other works might have deserv'd applause.

As Thomas Warton was to say, a hundred years later, after quoting this and similar testimony: 'I mention these descriptions of Milton, among many others of a like kind which appeared soon after his death, because they probably contain the tone of public opinion, and seem to represent the general and established estimation of his character at that time.'

Milton's friends were of course aware of the state of public opinion about him. This is amusingly illustrated by the story of Daniel Skinner Jr., as told in Masson's Life of Milton. Skinner, who had been a pupil and friend of Milton's for some time and one of his amanuenses, was admitted Junior Fellow of Trinity College, Cambridge, in October 1674, a month before Milton's death. In 1675 he was seeking public employment; he introduced himself to Pepys, and revealed to him that he had transcripts of Milton's Latin *Letters of State* and *De Doctrina Christiana*, which had been left him by the author, and for which he was negotiating publication by Daniel Elzevir of Amsterdam. In November Elzevir agreed to print the two manuscripts and shortly after they were in his hands. In October 1676 an edition of the *Letters of State* was published which, there can be little doubt, Edward Phillips was responsible for. Thereupon Skinner wrote to Sir Joseph Williamson, Secretary of State, drawing attention to this volume, published without authority, and asking for a licence to print his own copy. Sir Joseph however, in Skinner's words, 'was such an enemy to the name of Milton, he told me he could countenance nothing of that man's writings'. He asked Skinner to bring for his perusal what papers of Milton he had in his possession; Skinner did so, and at the same time presented a petition on his own behalf for some public employment. Sir Joseph received him graciously and promised his patronage. At this moment Skinner received the offer of an appointment to the English embassy at Nimeguen. On the day before he left he waited on Sir Joseph, who returned him his Milton papers and advised him not to proceed with the printing of them at Amsterdam; Skinner promised to recover them from Elzevir and 'suppress them for ever'. Sir Joseph however immediately wrote to Sir Leoline Jenkins, the English ambassador at Nimeguen, informing him that Skinner was coming there and commending him, but going on to say that he had mixed himself up in the ugly business of getting Milton's *Letters of State* published in Holland: 'I have told the young man what I thought of his mixing with that sort of men, and how taking such pitch is, and that indeed, till he had very well aired himself from such infectious a commerce as the friendship of Milton is, he could not be at all proper to touch any degree in the King's service.' When Skinner reached Nimeguen he was shown this letter and given to understand that he could not be employed until he was clear of this business, and so was sent to wait at Rotterdam. In a letter to Pepys of 19 November 1676, in which he tells of these happenings, Skinner begs him to persuade Sir Joseph to write again to Sir Leoline and to say that he is ready to dispose of the papers in any way either of them desires, 'and am so far from ever procuring a line from Milton printed that, if his honour pleases, he command my copies and all my other papers to the fire. And though I happened to be acquainted with Milton in his lifetime (which out of mere love to learning I procured, and no other concerns ever passed betwixt us but a great desire and ambition of some of his

[25]

learning), I am, and ever was, so far from being the least tainted with any of his principles that I may boldly say none has a greater honour and loyalty for his Majesty, more veneration for the Church of England, and love for his country, than I have.' On his father's orders Skinner now went to Paris. In March 1677 he received a letter from Dr. Isaac Barrow, Master of Trinity, ordering him to return to Cambridge at once on penalty of expulsion: 'We do also warn you that, if you shall publish any writing mischievous to the Church or State, you will thence incur a forfeiture of your interest here.' Skinner told the Master's messenger that, notwithstanding this command, he intended to go on to Italy that summer; and so he did. Meanwhile Elzevir had sent the manuscripts, wrapped in a paper parcel, to Skinner's father, who delivered them unopened to Sir Joseph. The parcel was put into a press in the old State Paper Office in Whitehall, and the *De Doctrina Christiana* was not seen or heard of again until the Deputy Keeper discovered it in 1825. On 23 May 1679 Daniel Skinner Jr. was 'sworn and admitted a major fellow' at Trinity College, Dr. Barrow being dead.

Let us turn from all this to the first three biographers who knew Milton. Naturally they were aware of the prejudice against him and of its causes, and naturally they tried to correct the portrait; but there are no signs that this influenced them to depart from the truth, and in Aubrey's case at least there was no reason why it should. Because Aubrey is a disinterested witness and because his Notes are brief and factual I shall use extracts from them as the basis for presenting the authentic portrait, adding extracts from the other early biographers where necessary. I fill out Aubrey's abbreviations.

Of the education of Milton's nephews:
'As he was severe on the one hand, so he was most familiar and free to those to whome most severe in his way of

education. – NB. He made his Nephews Songsters, and sing from the time they were with him.'

Of his first wife:

'He married his first wife . . . Powell of Fosthill in Oxonshire. She went without her husband's consent to her mother in the King's quarters (near Oxford). . . . By whom he had 4 children. . . . Deborah was his Amanuensis, he taught her Latin, and to read Greeke to him, when he had lost his eiesight.'

'His first wife (Mrs. Powell, a Royalist) was brought up and lived where there was a great deal of company & merriment, dancing &c., and when she came to live with her husband at Mr. Russell's in St. Bride's churchyard, she found it very solitary: no company came to her; . . . and so she went to her parents at Fosthill. He sent for her (after some time) and I think his servant was evil entreated.'

The return of his first wife (from Edward Phillips):

'. . . the then declining State of the King's Cause, and consequently of the Circumstances of *Justice* Powell's family, caused them to set all Enquiries on Work, to restore the Late Married Woman to the Station wherein they a little before had planted her; at last this device was pitch'd upon. There dwelt in the Lane of *St. Martin's Le Grand*, which was hard by, a Relation of our Author's, whom it was known he often visited. . . . One time above the rest, he making his usual visit, the Wife was ready in another Room, and on a sudden he was surprised to see one whom he had thought to have never seen more, making Submission and begging Pardon on her Knees before him; he might probably at first make shew of aversion and rejection; but partly his own generous nature, more inclinable to Reconciliation than to perseverance in Anger and Revenge, and partly the strong intercession of Friends on both sides, soon brought him to an Act of Oblivion, and a firm League of Peace for the future. . . . The first fruits of her return to her husband was a brave girl, born within a year after; . . . . But it was not only by Children that she increas'd the number of the Family, for in no very long time after her coming, she had a great resort of her Kindred with her in the House, *viz.* her Father and Mother, and Several of her Brothers and Sisters, which were in all pretty Numerous.'

Of his political opinions:

'Whatever he wrote against Monarchie was of no animosity to the King's person, but out of pure zeall to the Liberty of Mankind, which he thought would be greater under a free state than a Monarchall government.'

To this may be added the testimony of the anonymous biographer:

'And as hee was not link'd to one Party by self Interest, so was hee not divided from the other by Animosity; but was forward to do any of them good Offices, when their particular Cases afforded him ground to appeer on thir behalf. And especially if on the score of Witt or Learning, they could lay claim to his peculiar Patronage. Of which there were instances, among others, the Grand child of the famous Spencer, a Papist suffering in his concerns in Ireland, and Sr. William Davenant when taken Prisoner, for both of whom hee procur'd relief.'

Helen Darbishire points out that Milton's service to Davenant is corroborated by three other witnesses: by Anthony Wood in his Life of Davenant, who dates the incident 1651, by Jonathan Richardson, and by a letter of old Jacob Tonson's, who states that he was intimately acquainted with Davenant's second son:

'This Mr. Davenant told me that Mr. Milton helped him in his study of the Lattin and Greeke Authors, to whom he used to go in order to his Learning. – That when his father was in the tower he was very much assisted by Mr. Milton in his gaining his Liberty; and if I am not very much mistaken he at the same time told me that his father in return

[28]

upon the restoration was very helpfull to Milton, and Milton was very acknowledging for it and uppon that score offered his willingness in doing anything that should be grateful to Sr. William.'

Of his temper and habits:

'Of a very cheerful humour. He was very healthy, and free from all diseases, and only towards his later end he was visited with Gowte spring & Fall: he would be chearful even in his Gowte fits; and sing.'

'He was an early riser . . . yea after he lost his sight. He had a man to read to him: the first thing he read to him was the Hebrew Bible, and that was at 4 hours mane . . . . Then he contemplated. At 7 his man came to him again & then read to him & wrote till dinner: the writing was as much as the reading . . . to bed about nine. Temperate man, rarely drank between meales. Extreme pleasant in his conversation, & at dinner, supper, &c.: but satyrical. He pronounced the letter R very hard, a certain signe of a Satyricall wit (from John Dreyden).'

To this may be added what the anonymous biographer says of his habits of composition, and in illustration of his humour:

'And hee waking early (as is the use of temperate men) had commonly a good Stock of Verses ready against his Amanuensis came; which if it happened to be later than ordinary, hee would complain, Saying *hee wanted to bee milkd.*'

Of his friends and acquaintances in later life:

'He was mightily importuned to go into France and Itaile (foraigners came much to see him) & much admired him, and offered to him great preferments to come over to them, and the only inducement of severall foreigners that came over into England, was chiefly to see O. Protector & Mr. J. Milton, & would see the house & chamber wher he was borne: he was more admired abroad than at home. His familiar learned Acquaintance were Mr. Andrew Marvell,

[29]

Mr. Skinner, Dr. Pagett MD., . . . Mr. Skinner [Jr.] who
was his disciple, John Dreyden Esq. Poet Laureate, who
very much admires him, and went to him to have leave to
putt his Paradise-lost into a drama in rhyme: Mr. Milton
received him civilly, & told him he would give him leave to
tagge his Verses.'

Wood's Life, being the first to appear, became, as Warton
said, 'the first groundwork of all the lives of Milton'. Wood
follows his authorities, Aubrey and the anonymous biographer, closely; about half his life is taken almost verbatim
from the latter, and another tenth from Aubrey's Notes.
His other chief source is the autobiographical passages in
Milton's prose works, from which he takes a few additional
points. It is remarkable that, as a bigoted Monarchist and
Churchman, he is candid enough not to credit the calumnies
reported of Milton: 'he left the university of his own accord,
and was not expelled for misdemeanours, as his Adversaries
have said.' Nor does he withhold his admiration for Milton's
abilities. It was this air of candour, backed by authentic
knowledge, that gave his Life its effectual authority. Yet if
anyone had praised Wood for his candour he might have
replied as Dr. Johnson did when praised for his impartiality
in reporting the debates in the House of Commons: 'That
is not quite true: I saved appearances tolerably well, but
I took care that the Whig dogs should not have the best of
it.' Wood's is indeed a Tory Churchman's Life of Milton
and, although less fierce than Johnson's, is the prototype of
his.

What Wood does is to replace the intimate and pleasing
view of Milton given in his sources by a portrait consonant
with public sentiment about him. He does this partly by
substituting his own adverse comments for the apologetics of
his originals on Milton's public activities, partly by sup-
pressing or garbling or reversing what they say about him in
his private capacity. Wood's character of Milton is contained

in the longest of his more or less original passages: 'But
the times soon after changing, and the Rebellion thereupon breaking forth, Milton sided with the Faction, and
being a man of parts, was therefore more capable than
another of doing mischief, especially by his pen. . . . That
at first we find in him a Presbyterian and a sharp and most
violent opposer of Prelacy, the established ecclesiastical
Discipline and the orthodox Clergy. That shortly afterwards
he did set on foot and maintained very novel Positións con-
cerning divorce, and then taking part with the Indepen-
dents, he became a great Anti-monarchist, a bitter Enemy
to K. *Ch.* I, and at length arrived to that monstrous and
unparallel'd height of profligate impudence, as in print to
justify the most execrable murder of him the best of Kings,
as I shall anon tell you. Afterwards being made Latin
Secretary to the Parliament, we find him a Commonwealth
man, a hater of all things that looked towards a single
person, a great reproacher of the Universities, scholastical
degrees, decency, and uniformity in the Church. . . . That
when Oliver ascended the throne, he became the Latin
Secretary, and proved to him very serviceable when employed in business of weight and moment, and did great
matters to obtain a name and wealth. To conclude, he was
a man of wonderful parts, of a very sharp, biting, satyrical
wit. He was a good Philosopher and Historian, and excellent Poet, Latinist, Grecian, Hebritian, a good Mathema-
tician and Musitian, and so rarely endowed by nature, that
had he been but honestly principled, he might have been
highly useful to that party, against which he all along appeared with such malice and bitterness.' This, though much
more moderate than Johnson, gave Johnson his line.

One cannot object to Wood's representing the common
view of Milton's public activities, for he shared that view on
what were matters of public interest; one cannot even complain when he directly contradicts his authorities – as when

what the anonymous biographer says of *Clamor Regii Sanguinis* ('in which Salmasius was hugely extol'd, and Mr. Milton as falsely defam'd') is altered to, 'Salmasius was highly extolled, and Milton had his just character given therein.' It is easier for later scholars to correct a false impression of a public than of a private character. What one complains of, as I have said, is that he replaces the intimate portrait of the man so vividly given in his sources by a prejudiced portrait of the public man and his activities. He omits most of what they have to say about Milton at home, which is the essence of what they have to say; it is these omissions that account for his Life's being only two-thirds of the length of the Anonymous Life. Only rarely does he make a malicious addition to his authorities, as in his account of Milton's first marriage, which is taken verbatim from the anonymous biographer until at the end he makes it appear that Milton wrote the *Doctrine and Discipline of Divorce* after Mary's return and with a view to obtaining a judicial separation; and he can hardly be blamed for this, since a similar mistake went uncontradicted for over two centuries. And at the same time he does quote the anonymous biographer's words, that Milton showed 'gentleness and humanity . . . in receiving home, and living in good accord till her death with his first wife'. Honest man that he was however, it was Anthony Wood who, in Newman's words, 'poisoned the wells of truth'.

It remains to add something from Jonathan Richardson, since he is a fresh voice from the younger generation and since it was he who provoked Johnson's attack on Milton's character. One's sole complaint against Richardson is his garrulity. He states his purpose plainly in his opening words: 'If I can give a more Exact and a more Just idea of *Milton,* and of *Paradise Lost,* than the Public has yet had of Either, I am Assured it will be Acceptable to all Honest and Ingenuous Minds of What Party Soever.' Later he

remarks that Milton 'does Now, and has Long Since Shone
in the Eyes of the Generality of the World, rather as a
Great Poet, than as a Good Man'. Again: 'I fear it will be
to little Purpose if I proceed on *Milton's* Moral or Religious,
'till I have quenched or abated the Prejudices of Most of
my Readers with Regard to his Political Character. . . . Not
only his Political Principles have been Censur'd, but his
Behaviour under them as Virulent, and Dishonest.' He adds
that although 'after the Restoration, he no more engaged in
the Old Disputes . . . even Now he Scorn'd to Flatter
Power, as Many did; the Same Openness and Honesty was
seen in him, his Old Principles were known to continue,
they are seen even in *Paradise Lost*'.

When he comes to the domestic scandals he shows him-
self both robust and humane:
'Now that I am upon This Sort of Work, to Brush off more
Dirt . . . and the rather, because he has no where done it
Himself that I know of, perhaps as being a Domestick
Affair, or perhaps he Never Suspected his Garment Had, or
would have any Such Spot on it. I don't remember to have
ever heard he was Sour, or Morose in General, and in
Common Life, but the Contrary. . . . Affability and Good
Nature was his General Character. The Charge I am Now
to Speak to is, that Whatever he was Elsewhere, How
Patiently soever he bore the Provocations Two of his Wives
gave him. . . . Yet that he was too Rigid a Master of his
Family; but More Especially, That he was a Severe and
Cruel Father . . . but there is One very Particular Instance
of Severity he is Charg'd with . . . what I mean, is his
Compelling Two of his Daughters to Learn to Read,
without Understanding One Word, Several Languages,
and to Read To, and Write For him Continually. I speak
here of Two Thus Employ'd, though Some say but One,
She that dy'd a few Years Since, and was so much Spoke of
and Visited, and So Nobly Reliev'd for His Sake. . . . Such

[33]

is the Byas towards the Young People . . . if Any thing is Amiss, and the Question is Whether the Father or the Children are to Blame, All, or the Greater Part falls to the Share of the Old Man. Would to God I could produce *Milton*, his Own Advocate on the Present, as on Other Occasions. . . . He Probably would have put These Busy-Bodies in Mind of the Spanish Proverb, *A Fool is Wiser in his Own House, than a Wise Man in That of his Neighbour* . . . but admitting it was a Hardship; let the Father be taken into Account, let Some regard be had to Him. Here was an Old Man, Blind, Infirm, near Ruin'd, Afflicted; Standing in great Need therefore of Assistance from Those of Whom he had reason to Expect it, and of what Consolation They could Afford; One of the Principal Branches of which was Reading, and Writing for him . . . and was it Nothing (think ye) no Hardship upon Him to Teach Girls as These were Taught? Consider His Distress Either way; and Pity Him you have been Blaming. . . . Only let Me add, that That Daughter . . . that was Thus Serviceable to her Excellent Father in his Distress, Express'd no Uneasiness, that I ever heard of, when she gave Accounts of Milton's Affairs to the Many Enquirers Lately; but on the Contrary, spoke of him with Great Tenderness; particularly I have been told She said He was Delightful Company, the Life of the Conversation, and That on Account of a Flow of Subject, and an Unaffected Chearfulness and Civility. One Instance of her Tender Remembrance of Him I cannot forbear relating. The Picture in Crayons I have of him was Shown her after several Others, or which were Pretended to be His; when Those were shown and She was Asked if She could recollect if She had ever seen Such a Face. No, No. but when This was Produc'd, in a Transport, – 'tis My Father, 'tis my Dear Father; I see him! 'tis Him! And then She put her Hands to several Parts of Her Face, 'tis the very Man! Here, Here – .'

Richardson's main point is given in the following words: 'Such who . . . have Suffer'd what They have been Taught, or Chosen to Dislike in him, to Eclipse him, so as that, though they See him to be a great Poet, they look on him as Shining with a Sort of Disastrous Light, will, if they possess Good Minds, Rejoice in finding a Character Amiably Bright, where they Expected no Such; and will perhaps Read Him with More Delight, and Enrich their Own Minds the more by So doing, than if Themselves had continu'd Labouring under their Old Prejudices.' That *Paradise Lost* has suffered from dislike of Milton the man is borne out in the history of Milton criticism; yet there was no time when this was less so than when Richardson published his 'Remarks'. He had grown up in a period when Milton was generally reviled, and therefore saw it as necessary to defend the man to save the poet; yet the feeling against Milton had in fact already died down in 1734, and Richardson was contending against a public opinion that belonged rather to the last quarter of the seventeenth century. Fenton's Life of Milton, published nine years earlier, reveals no such consciousness of the need to save his author from the effects of prejudice; still less does Thomas Newton's, published fourteen years later. The eighteenth-century biographers are of course aware of the facts, but only as past history; to them they are 'old, unhappy, far-off things, and battles long ago'. It was Dr. Johnson who put the fat in the fire again.

Johnson's Life was begun in January 1779 and finished in six weeks. Malone reports that on 5 April 1779, 'Johnson told me, "We have had too many honeysuckle Lives of Milton, and that his should be of another strain." ' Helen Darbishire has suggested that Johnson was thinking chiefly of Fenton's Life. But Johnson says in his Life of Milton, 'I might have contented myself with the addition of a few notes to Fenton's elegant Abridgement'; and in his Life of

Fenton he speaks of his 'short and elegant account of Milton's life, written at once with integrity and tenderness'. Johnson consulted the lives by Wood, Edward Phillips, Toland, Bayle, Fenton, Richardson, Birch and Newton; but the one he was thinking of when he spoke to Malone of honeysuckle lives was Richardson's, whom in his Life of Milton he calls 'the fondest of his [Milton's] admirers', and says that he 'seems to have been very diligent in his enquiries, but discovers a wish to find Milton discriminated from other men'. Johnson was determined to stop this nonsense. As a good Tory and Churchman he set himself to depict Milton in the old colours once again, as the sour republican and rebel. It was he who revived the original prejudiced view and painted the portrait that has ever since been accepted for true.

That Johnson's Life was a shock to contemporary feeling can be seen in a letter of Cowper's written at the end of October of the same year: 'His treatment of Milton is unmerciful to the last degree. A pensioner is not likely to spare a republican; and the Doctor, in order, I suppose, to convince his royal patron of the sincerity of his monarchical principles, has belaboured that great poet's character with the most industrious cruelty. If he had any virtues, they are not to be found in the Doctor's picture of him.' He concludes with one of the most delightful outbursts in literature: 'Oh! I could thresh his old jacket, till I made his pension jingle in his pocket.' There is no scene one would have better liked to witness than that of Cowper snatching the burly Doctor's oaken staff to chastise him with.

Johnson worked with all the available Lives open before him, taking each point in turn and making his caustic comments. I will quote enough to recall the total picture.

Of Milton's years at Cambridge:
'There is reason to believe that he was regarded in his college with no fondness.'

Of Milton's saying that he was 'Church-outed by the Prelates':

'These expressions are I find applied to the subscription of the Articles, but it seems more probable that they relate to canonical obedience . . . the thoughts of obedience, whether canonical or civil, raised his indignation.'

Milton as controversialist:

'. . . scarcely ever any man wrote so much and praised so few. . . . Sometimes he tries to be humorous . . . his gloomy seriousness is yet more offensive. Such is his malignity that hell grows darker at his frown.'

Of his pretentions to patriotic motives in returning from Italy:

'Let not our veneration for Milton forbid us to look with some degree of merriment on great promises and small performance, on the man who hastens home because his countrymen are contending for liberty, and, when he reaches the scene of action, vapours away his patriotism in a private boarding school.'[1]

Of Mary Powell's desertion:

'Milton was too busy to much miss his wife. . . . At last Michaelmas arrived; but the lady had no inclination to return to the sullen gloom of her husband's habitation. . . . In a man whose opinion of his own merit was like Milton's, less provocation than this might have raised violent resentment . . . and, being one of those who could easily find arguments to justify his inclinations, published *The Doctrine and Discipline of Divorce*.'

Later Johnson reluctantly shows his normal candour in quoting Edward Phillips on Milton's reconciliation with his wife:

'It were injurious to omit, that Milton afterwards received

[1] On this see my article, *The Alleged Falsehood In Milton's Account of His Continental Tour*, (M.L.R., July 1933).

her father and her brother in his own home, when they were
distressed, with other Royalists.'

Of Milton's second marriage:

'About this time his first wife died in childbed. . . . As he
probably did not love her he did not long continue the
appearance of lamenting her . . . but after a short time
married Catherine . . . a woman doubtless educated in
opinions like his own. She died within a year of childbirth,
or some distemper that followed it; and her husband has
honoured her memory with a poor sonnet.'

The tone of this beautiful poem, 'Methought I saw my late
espoused saint', is sufficient answer to Johnson's coarse
remarks, which are supported by no evidence at all. R. W.
Parker has suggested that the sonnet was written on the
death of his first wife, but whilst there is nothing incredible
in this on personal grounds it is less likely than the usual
ascription. Mary died in May 1652, when Milton was
already blind; he married Katharine Woodcock 22 October
1656. Over four years is not 'a short time' for a blind man
with three young daughters to stay unmarried.

Of Milton as political turncoat:

'From this time it is to be observed that he became an
enemy of the Presbyterians, whom he had favoured before.
He that changes his party by his humour is not more
virtuous than he that changes it by his interest; he loves
himself rather than the truth.'

At Cromwell's assumption of absolute power:

'Milton, having now tasted the honey of public employment,
would not return to hunger and philosophy, but, continuing
to exercise his office under a manifest usurpation, betrayed
to his power that liberty which he had defended. Nothing
can be more just than that rebellion should end in slavery.'

Of Milton's pardon after the Restoration:

'Milton, now being cleared of all the effects of his dis-
loyalty, had nothing required of him but the common duty

of living in quiet, to be rewarded with the common right of protection; but this, which, when he skulked from the approach of his King, was perhaps more than he hoped, seems not to have satisfied him, for no sooner is he safe than he finds himself in danger, "fallen on evil days and evil tongues, and with darkness and with danger compassed round".'

As we have seen, Milton retired into private life after the Restoration, to complete the poem from which Johnson quotes.

And here is Johnson's final character of Milton:

'His political notions were those of an acrimonious and surly republican. . . . Milton's republicanism was, I am afraid, founded on an envious hatred of greatness, and a sullen desire of independence; in petulance impatient of control, and pride disdainful of superiority. He hated monarchs in the state and prelates in the church; for he hated all whom he was required to obey. It is to be suspected that his predominate desire was to destroy rather than to establish, and that he felt not so much love of liberty as repugnance to authority. It has been observed that they who most loudly clamour for liberty do not liberally grant it. What we know of Milton's character and domestick relations is, that he was severe and arbitrary. His family consisted of women; and there appears in his books something like a Turkish contempt of females, as subordinate and inferior beings. . . . He thought woman made only for obedience, and man only for rebellion.'

All this is Johnson at his doughtiest. He however, unlike so many since, does not make the mistake of allowing his dislike of the man to affect his judgment of the poet: there has been no nobler praise of *Paradise Lost* than his. Gerard Manley Hopkins too thought Milton 'a bad man' but admired him as a poet.

The final stroke in the denigration of Milton was given

[39]

by one of his most devoted admirers, when Masson observed that the *Doctrine and Discipline of Divorce* was published in July 1643 and must therefore, according to the traditional dating of Milton's first marriage, have been written during his honeymoon. I succeeded in showing (*Modern Language Review*, October 1931 and January 1932) that this traditional date for the marriage, Whitsuntide 1643, had been read into Edward Phillips's account by Toland, and that every scrap of evidence shows the marriage to have taken place a year earlier. But the damage had been done, and the ludicrous story is still credited by many, at least as *ben trovato*.

There is no need to insist that Johnson's view of Milton's life and character is the one that still prevails, since every schoolboy is taught it and most adults hold by it as gospel truth. I have no wish to replace it by an 'honeysuckle' view; I plead only for something more agreeable with the evidence. Many will continue to find Milton an unsympathetic character even when they have rid themselves of the libels about him – strong but proud, stiff in opinion and overbearing, too stern to be amiable. That will not matter because it will not altogether misrepresent the poet; the excitement of his poetry, as of Dante's, often comes from the sternness, what some will think the harshness, of his judgments. And anyone who attends to the poetry without prejudice may come to notice, as with Dante, not only the sternness but the pity, the gentleness and humanity beneath.

Chapter 2

THE MORAL IN THE FABLE

In examining the poem one of my main purposes will be to follow the development of the story and the ways in which the poet's ideas are presented through it. The characters, scenes and incidents, the diction, verse, and imagery, can only be profitably discussed in connexion with the unfolding of the action as an embodiment of the ideas.

The story told in *Paradise Lost* of the creation and fall of man, with all its doctrinal bearings on the riddle of the universe, has to be accepted by us as it was by Milton and his age. If it is found no longer philosophically or scientifically convincing it must nevertheless be accepted for the time being. We are concerned not with its absolute or its historical truth but with its poetic truth as embodied in the narrative; and we must go along with the poet in his telling of a story he himself accepted as perfect truth. This is a critical truism, yet how many accept it in the case of *Paradise Lost*?

I shall deal only with certain of his theological ideas and with his views on married love, which are crucial to the poem. Many put the theology on one side in order to read the poem, as they say, as poetry. But theology was the very soul of his poem for Milton. This is a theological epic, the whole purpose of which is 'to assert Eternal Providence, and justifie the ways of God to men'; and it is impossible to overlook the theology without overlooking the poetry, or at least misreading it.

We must not of course examine the theology as a thing

apart, as if it were Milton's prose treatise, *De Doctrina Christiana*. The *De Doctrina* can be used to elucidate the ideas behind the poem but we are concerned with them only as they stand in the poem, as they are expressed there and have their bearings on the action. If there is any theology that has not been converted into poetry, that remains undigested theology, this must be noted as a poetic fault; but it will be found that there are fewer such faults in the poem than is usually thought, if only we go along with the poet. We must appreciate too that this theology is a complete theological system, the Christian interpretation of human history. It is not the modern way of thought, which since the seventeenth century has become increasingly governed by natural science. But in order to read the poem *Paradise Lost* we must try to think in the theological terms of the seventeenth century, just as we must think in pagan terms in order to read Homer and Virgil, or of Epicurean philosophy in order to read Lucretius, or of Thomist theology in order to read Dante, or of nineteenth-century mechanistic thought in order to read Thomas Hardy.

It is, however, necessary to note the difference between Milton's attitude to his story, the way he believes in it, and that of the ancient epic or dramatic poets to theirs. The difference is especially clear in the case of *Samson Agonistes*, where the given story is the perfect 'objective correlative' of Milton's beliefs and ideas, in a manner in which perhaps none of the fables of the ancient Greek tragedies were. It is this difference that gives Milton's great religious poems their uniqueness. Nothing really like them had ever been written before; no poem in the classical epic form had been written with this complete 'sincerity', and none has been written since. The result is that the epic form allows Milton to express his entire mind. It is more than a question of his being free to use all the material accumulated during the long years of preparation for the poem, of deploying to the full extent his learning and experience; it is a question of his being able to write out in full his account of life. For this is the proper task of the epic poet: to present a comprehensive view, a conspectus of life, as it appears to him and his times. In presenting this total view, this complete survey and interpretation of life, he will necessarily present a system of thought, a philosophy or theology. The objection that has sometimes been brought against *Paradise Lost*, that it presents a scheme of life instead of life itself (whatever life itself is), is therefore a misdirected criticism, unless the scheme has not been embodied in and borne out by the story. The reason why the Romantic poets, Wordsworth and Shelley and Keats, failed in their attempts to write an epic, was that they had to invent both the philosophy and the fable; and it is doubtful whether this double task is within the scope of the greatest genius. It is significant that Byron, with his satiric and devil-may-care *Don Juan*, came nearest to success. It is not until a faith has attained practically universal acceptance within its own boundaries and has produced its own fit fables, that it is ready for the epic poet. The first Book of *The Prelude* tells how Wordsworth failed to find a fable suited to his modern thought and so had to fall back on the Romantic's substitute of the autobiographical, telling the story of 'The Growth of a Poet's Mind' as a means of giving his account of life. *The Dynasts*, the last of our epics, uses the Napoleonic wars to present Hardy's ironic conception of the universe, controlled and directed not by intelligent superior powers but by blind unconscious forces; a view of life that represented the view of an important and growing section of the serious-minded people of his time. It was a titanic effort, but one reason why it may be held to be inferior to *Paradise Lost* as an epic is that it does not represent a catholic faith but is a special reading of history. The fable and moral agree only for those of Hardy's sect.

[43]

Insofar then as Milton has succeeded in his task he has presented a total view of life that existed as a catholic faith in the Christendom of his day; and has presented it through a fable that grew up with that faith and expresses it exactly. The grand scheme of the poem is to tell the Christian story of God's purposes towards man; to present the relation of the created world, of which this earth is the centre, to the infinite and eternal; to show this earth with its depravity, misery and folly, as well as its capabilities of beauty, goodness, heroism and love, as the outcome of the contending powers of good and evil in the universe; and so to justify the ways of God to men. To many today it is no longer convincing as an explanation but Milton's poetic success depended on his believing it, as does our appreciation of the poem.

The first thing to realise about the theology of *Paradise Lost* is that it is entirely catholic doctrine, using 'catholic' in its proper sense. It was only after the discovery of the *De Doctrina Christiana*, with its heterodoxies, that readers began to look for the presence of these heterodoxies in the poem; there is now a reaction against this attitude. What we find is that, while there is nothing in the poem that contradicts what we know from the *De Doctrina* of Milton's peculiar beliefs, there is also nothing that need offend the orthodox Christian; as a poet Milton had the sense to be judicious in this respect. He wrote what all Christians in his own day and down to Dr. Johnson's could read without suspecting heresy, and there is no reason why we should not read it in the same way; after all we know less about Christian theology than the seventeenth century, and care less about heresies. We are concerned with the theology not as theology but as an integral part of the poetry, and any heresies the poem may contain need not trouble us so long as they do not disturb the poetic vision.

Such a disturbing of the poetic vision is the sole ground,

as Pope saw, for objecting to Milton's God. Treating his
subject in the form of the classical epic it was necessary that
God should appear as a character in the poem; Heaven is an
essential phase of the action, and if Heaven is to be presented
so must God be. Waldock thought that Milton should have
presented God in Dante's manner – indirectly, obliquely,
by what Henry James called the principle of 'delegated
sensibility'. But this is exactly what Milton does; his God
remains a mystery, no more than a presence. The note is
struck at once in the prologue to Book III:

> since God is Light,
> And never but in unapproached Light
> Dwelt from Eternitie, . . .   [iii. 3–5

God is seen only in reflected glory in his Creation in Heaven
and Earth; he himself is a voice, his person invisible and
unknowable. But he is fully manifest in the 'Divine Similitude' of the Son,

> In whose conspicuous count'nance, without cloud
> Made visible, th' Almighty Father shines,
> Whom else no Creature can behold.   [iii. 385–7

Similarly Milton solves the problem of showing God in
action (another necessity of epic narrative) by means of the
orthodox doctrine that the Father acts through the Son; and
he is invariably successful in showing the Son in action –
riding into battle against the rebel angels, going forth to
and returning from the Creation, summoning Adam and
Eve to judgment in the Garden, and presenting their mute
prayers to God after their repentance.

Milton thus surmounts the difficulty of presenting God
both as a figure and as an actor in the poem, which he is
not usually given credit for; his God is spoken of as an
unqualified failure. The fact is that it is only God as revealed in some of his speeches, and the echoes of these in the

[45]

poet's own comments, which we rightly object to. Pope has expressed it in a single line:

> And God the Father turns a School-Divine.

The poet's error is to make God argue and justify himself when he should have made him only pronounce. The belief that truth of dogma can be demonstrated to the reason is as characteristic of Milton as of anyone in that rationalistic century; it is a habit of mind inherited from the medieval schoolmen whom Milton claimed to despise. To us it is the unpoetic side of his mind, and it certainly has unfortunate poetic results in *Paradise Lost*. It at once brings in question that absoluteness of God which the poet asserts. There can be no finality in an argument; and it is not surprising in the circumstances that Satan should be thought to have the best of the argument. Once this doubt is allowed to arise all sorts of false issues follow, which the author can only deal with ineffectually by further argument. The role that God should fulfil in the poem is that of an absolute monarch, which is how Milton does in fact describe and show him. His speeches should have consisted of unargued dogma and decree; these are necessary parts of the action – the action indeed depends on them – and they cannot be given on the authority of anyone but God. But argument about them should have been left to the other characters, and particularly to Satan and his companions. The reader would have accepted dogma where he is now unconvinced by reasoning; and dogma would then have played its appropriate part in the poem.

Now that this fault has been discussed we can proceed to Milton's ideas as they belong to the action and to the total imaginative effect at which he aimed. I shall use the *Christian Doctrine* for a clear statement of these theological ideas and beliefs. One of his fundamental beliefs is that all things belong to God and are a unity in him. Since God is all in all,

all things therefore proceed from him (including the material Creation) and remain a part of his nature forever. God cannot, he says, 'properly be called infinite if he is capable of receiving any accession whatever, which would be the case if anything could exist in the nature of things which had not first been of God and in God.' Therefore not only the ethereal substance out of which God created the Heavens and the angels but also the matter out of which he created man and his universe must have originated from God and be a part of God. This original matter from which he made man and his world 'is not to be looked on as an evil or trivial thing but as intrinsically good, and the chief productive stock of every subsequent good' (sc. in this world). '. . . It was a substance derivable from no other source than the fountain of every substance. . . . Like the form and nature of the Angels it proceeded incorruptible from God; and ever since the Fall it remains incorruptible as far as concerns its essence.' This belief is the basis of Milton's fundamental optimism, his faith in the final redemption of man and his world.

A corollary Milton draws from this belief in the oneness of things in God is that there can be no real and final distinction between the material and the spiritual. There is for example no ultimate distinction between body and soul, since they are of one substance in God: 'Man is a living being . . . one and individual, not compound or separable, not, according to the common opinion, made up and framed of two distinct and different natures, as of soul and body . . . but a single substance, individual, animated, sensitive and rational.' At death therefore the whole man dies, body and soul, and at the Resurrection the whole man, body and soul, will be raised from the tomb. Similarly there can be no absolute division between men and angels on the one hand or between men and lower forms of life on the other. Raphael tells Adam that angels have incorporeal forms

[47]

corresponding in all their functions to human bodies, and

contain
Within them every lower facultie
Of sense, whereby they hear, see, smell, touch, taste, . . .
[v. 409–11

And before relating the war in Heaven he tells him,

what surmounts the reach
Of human sense, I shall delineate so,
By lik'ning spiritual to corporeal forms,
As may express them best: though what if Earth
Be but the shaddow of Heav'n, and things therein
Each to other like, more than on Earth is thought?
[v. 571–6

Dr. Johnson found fault with the effects of this doctrine in
Milton's presentation of his supernatural characters in the
war in Heaven: 'He has unfortunately perplexed his poetry
with his philosophy. His infernal and celestial powers are
sometimes pure spirit and sometimes animated body. . . .
The confusion of spirit and matter that pervades the whole
narration of the war in heaven fills it with incongruity.'
I shall defer answering this criticism until we come to the
episode in its place in the poem.

There is another consequence of this doctrine that all
things proceeded incorruptible from God. As originally
created, man and his world were ruled by inherent goodness;
they moved in natural obedience to God. This is the state
of nature in Eden before the Fall. In *The Christian Doctrine*
Milton states that by nature and the law of nature we
should not understand those physical laws whereby God is
thought to uphold the order of nature as an external agent,
but the natural obedience to God's will of what is essentially
a part of himself: 'for nature cannot mean anything but the
mysterious power and efficacy of that divine word which
went forth in the beginning and to which, as a perpetual

command, all things have since paid obedience.' In the mind of man this law of nature becomes conscious and is called reason. The terms 'reason' and 'right reason' recur perpetually in *Paradise Lost,* and always in this sense of the human mind moving in natural obedience to God's will; this it is 'which enables man to discern the chief good and in which consists, as it were, the life of the understanding'. After the Fall this power of reason is weakened but not destroyed. He could have read all this in Hooker's *Laws of Ecclesiastical Polity* as well as in other authors ancient and modern; it was a commonplace of the time.

But how in such a state of perfect goodness did the Fall ever happen? This is the ultimate problem of theology and of all other philosophies – the problem of the origin of evil; and it can receive only a dogmatic answer. In Christian historiography the problem goes back to the Fall of the angels. Milton's answer, put, as so much of his theological dogma is, into God's mouth, relies on the doctrine of Free Will. Satan and his followers fell of their own free will:

> Freely they stood who stood, and fell who fell.
> Not free, what proof could they have giv'n sincere
> Of true allegiance, constant Faith or Love,
> Where only what they needs must do, appear'd,
> Not what they would? [iii. 102–6

The argument appears to be that God himself permits the possibility of evil as a test of obedience. In Book V Adam, comforting Eve after her strange dream, is made to say,

> Evil into the mind of God or Man
> May come and go, so unapprov'd, and leave
> No spot or blame behind. [v. 117–19

'God' is probably used here as in other places for 'Angel'; and the meaning would then be that all God's creatures,

[49]

even angels, are liable to temptation. God however states a distinction between the Fall of the angels and man:

> The first sort by thir own suggestion fell,
> Self-tempted, self-deprav'd: Man falls deceiv'd
> By th' other first: Man therefore shall find grace,
> The other none.   [iii. 129–32

Of the occasion provided for man's temptation – the fruit of the Tree of Knowledge – Milton gives this explanation in *The Christian Doctrine*: 'It was necessary that something should be forbidden or commanded as a test of fidelity, and that an act in its own nature indifferent, in order that man's obedience might be thereby manifested. For since it was the disposition of man to do right, as being naturally good and holy, it was not necessary that he should be bound by the obligation of a covenant to perform that to which he was himself inclined; nor would he have given any proof of obedience by the performance of works to which he was led by a natural impulse, independently of the divine command. . . . This command formed no part of the law of nature, which is sufficient of itself to teach whatever is agreeable to right reason, that is to say whatever is intrinsically good. Such a command must therefore have been founded on what is called positive right, whereby God . . . commands or forbids what is in itself neither good nor bad.' In the poem the apple is similarly treated as a simple symbol of obedience for those who by nature were incapable of disobedience to God. The triviality of the offence for which man is condemned leads Satan, however, and others since, to represent God as a tyrant and to question his justice.

Milton's conception of divine justice is firmly and unequivocally expressed in the poem. Foretelling man's disobedience and its consequences, God says,

> Hee with his whole posteritie must die,
> Die hee or Justice must.   [iii. 209–10

And after Adam and Eve have fallen and repented of their
sin, and God has received their prayers for forgiveness, he
says,

> But longer in that Paradise to dwell,
> The Law I gave to Nature him forbids.
>
> [xi. 48–49

Such unrelenting justice revolts the modern sentimentalist;
he finds it incompatible with his idea of a loving, merciful,
forgiving God. But as John Lawlor argues in *The Tragic
Sense in Shakespeare*, discussing this same question in regard
to *Lear*, justice 'has nothing directly to do with repentance
and forgiveness'. Justice is the aim and purpose of law, its
sole principle; it is absolute, and its action irrevocable. Just
as we are automatically punished if we offend against a law
of physical nature, so are we punished for offending against
a moral law. There is no appeal, no reprieve; the law must
take its course. To suppose that because God is omnipotent
he can disregard his own decrees, suspend his own laws,
is to think him a tyrant indeed. He is an absolute monarch
but law-abiding: otherwise 'chaos is come again'. God's
mercy operates through his grace and not by abrogation of
his law of nature. The difference between Shakespeare and
Milton in this matter is that in drama such abstract ideas
must remain implicit whereas in narrative poetry they may
be stated. It is chiefly on account of this conception of
divine justice that Milton's whole religious thinking has
been called legalistic; it is not legalistic but lawful, and
those who reject it are in fact asking for an unlawful,
anarchic world.

There is one other general idea we need to take into
account, which is implicit in these theological doctrines,
though not itself entirely theological. This is the conception
of universal subordination. A word will suffice to explain it,
since it has become a commonplace which many have

expounded as a dominant Elizabethan conception. Like so many ruling ideas of the Renaissance it derives from the Middle Ages, though it is adapted to the different political and intellectual conditions of the Tudor and Stuart periods. It is a sort of feudal conception of the whole creation. There is a scale of being extending right down from the arch-angels to the plants and minerals of this earth; the universe is a unity in which everything has its place or degree, and is dependent on that which is next above it. To rebel against this divine order, whether it be the revolt of angels or men, or the revolt of subjects against their lawful king, is to bring in chaos again; it is the origin of all the evils of the world. As applied to politics the Puritans altered its bearings by claiming that everyone owed obedience not to an earthly but to an heavenly king; but as a cosmic or theological doctrine they accepted it, as does Milton. As an interpretation of the Fall it goes back at least to Augustine: man, like Satan, rebelled against God and that was the cause of the corruption of his nature and his world, under which we still suffer.

It is by all these ideas that we must interpret the story of *Paradise Lost* and its characters, especially those of Satan, Adam and Eve. For the chief function of the characters in a story, as Aristotle knew, is to express the action; and the action includes, besides the characters, the moral or meaning, or what Milton and his contemporaries called the argument, of the poem. Weak-minded moderns shy away from such words, and think they get clear of them by using longer ones, such as 'psychological' for 'moral'. I shall be plain and say that we cannot understand Satan for instance unless we understand his moral situation.

Much perverse nonsense has been talked about Milton's Satan because critics have refused to listen to the poet's plain words about his character and conduct and moral situation, preferring to concentrate on his heroic and romantic aspects, and so missing the true greatness of Milton's creation. Satan is the enemy of God and man. That is his role in the story, and he must be equal to his role as the adversary of the omnipotent. He must be granted the virtues and the powers to play his part as the Archfiend; he must be seen as a towering genius: but we must never be allowed to forget that his genius is Satanic. All his virtues are in fact corrupted by his situation and by the uses to which he puts his powers.

The original sin of Satan is the same as man's: disobedience to God. The motive from which he acted was pride – the orthodox Christian view. There are many who think Satan's pride is a reflection of Milton's own, that Milton unconsciously sympathizes with him, and that Satan therefore is his real hero. I shall not spend time on this nonsense, which Charles Williams, for one, has exploded. Satan's pride makes him declare himself equal to God. It is this inordinate sense of his own importance that governs all his conduct and it makes him irretrievably evil.

We shall not be likely to misread the story if this fact is kept in mind – that Satan and his fellows are evil – remembering it not as a doctrinal point but as a fact determining their whole situation, their actions and words at every stage. They differ from men in that they are incapable of repentance; they are lost souls 'to whom hope never comes, that comes to all'. It is summed up at the end of Satan's opening soliloquy in Book IV: 'Evil be thou my Good'.

Satan and his fellows are desperate creatures. It is an human instinct to admire the courage of despair and chivalrous devotion to a lost cause; such courage Satan has, and such chivalry he seems to have, and they have always attracted the admiration of readers. To simple-minded moderns, untrained in theological speculation, this admiration seems only right and proper. But Milton knew and repeatedly tells us that all Satan's words and deeds were perverse and vain. It was a common elementary idea then, but it flies over our heads. Many insist on regarding Satan as a Byronic hero, or give him all the credit for courage and endurance and leadership that they do to a 'pius Aeneas' and other worthy epic heroes; they do not understand, they will not even listen when the poet says there is no merit in all this. If we are to understand Milton's Satan we must cease regarding him as a great unfortunate: this of course he is, like Macbeth, and like Macbeth he is wicked and unrepentant to the end. This makes him a great tragic figure; but although Milton first planned *Paradise Lost* as a tragedy it is not, as we have it, a tragedy but an epic. The neoclassical theory of the 'forms' is not just pedantry; a writer ignores it at his peril. To regard Satan as the hero of Milton's epic is to stultify the poet's whole intention; if he is the hero then *Paradise Lost* is a bad poem, since Milton will have failed to express its meaning through the hero — and by its meaning I mean what Milton meant and not what some critic supposes him to have meant.

On Satan as a tragic character I refer readers to Helen Gardner's 'Milton and the Tragedy of Damnation' (*English Studies*, 1948). She resolves the controversy between the Satanists and anti-Satanists, between those who thought with Blake and Shelley and Byron, and those who thought with Charles Williams and his followers; between those who saw Satan as the *raison d'être* of the poem and those who saw him more or less as a figure-of-fun like the devil in a medieval play. Both parties to the dispute were half right and half wrong. Satan appeals to human feeling as a great tragic figure; and though everyone must be sensible of that appeal we cannot feel it to the full, as the poet presents him, unless we realise that, like Marlowe's Faustus and Shakespeare's Macbeth, he is not only wicked but utterly and irretrievably damned.

All this might not have needed pointing out, since Milton makes it clear, were it not for the foolish notion that he is lacking in dramatic ability and that therefore the words he puts into his character's mouth are to be taken as expressing the poet's own opinions. It is the sort of critical stupidity which in *Defensio Prima* Milton accuses Salmasius of.

A further word has to be said on the paradoxical view that Satan is the hero of *Paradise Lost*. This appears true only if we accept the traditional epic idea of the hero as a great warrior and leader. But Milton, as he stresses everywhere in the poem, had a very different idea of the heroic. In the prologue to Book IX he states this view explicitly:

> Since first this Subject for Heroic Song
> Pleas'd me long choosing, and beginning late;
> Not sedulous by Nature to indite
> Warrs, hitherto the onely Argument
> Heroic deemd, chief maistrie to dissect
> With long and tedious havoc fabl'd Knights
> In Battels feignd; the better fortitude
> Of Patience and Heroic Martyrdom
> Unsung.   [ix. 25-33

The 'long and tedious havoc' of this sort of heroic story, in the *Iliad* and the *Aeneid* and the chivalric romances, is represented in *Paradise Lost* by the satiric episode of the war in Heaven. The 'better fortitude of Patience and Heroic Martyrdom' is represented most obviously by Christ, suffering for the sins of the world; but in the story it is represented more immediately by the fallen Adam after repentance. The hero as martyr, who suffers patiently and refuses to the death to renounce his God, is the central idea of *Paradise Regain'd* and *Samson Agonistes* as well as of *Paradise Lost*. His idea of the heroic, along with his own heroic temper, is what puts Milton among the great poets of the world.

The last of Milton's main ideas in *Paradise Lost* I shall deal with is his view of wedded love. Because he wrote only of wedded love the author of *Paradise Lost* has never been thought of as a love poet. Most, when they speak of love poetry, think of lyrical poetry addressed by a lover to his mistress. Milton's early love poetry in this kind is in Latin and Italian, and this again effectively puts him out of court for most modern readers. Three of the Latin elegies belong to this class of personal love poetry, the commonest kind of poetry in the sixteenth and seventeenth centuries. Written between the ages of eighteen and twenty-one, they treat of sexual love in the frank and ardent manner of the Latin elegists, though, as Hanford observed, without the indecency to be found in them. The main section of *Elegy V* for instance is a voluptuous description of the Earth welcoming the return of the sun: 'Thus the wanton Earth breathes her amorous desires, and all her children haste to follow her lead.' Similarly the Italian sonnets are the record of an early love affair, probably written, as J. S. Smart showed, about the age of twenty-one. Here as in the Latin elegies he used a foreign language to reveal personal emotions and experiences he would have thought it unbecoming to express in English. As anyone writing Latin elegies must write love poems in the manner of Ovid and the other ancient poets, because this was the form for such poetry, so anyone writing Italian sonnets was expected to write after the manner of Petrarch to Laura. Nevertheless these poems reveal a side of his nature usually ignored, because they represent it insulated by a literary convention, in the first case from Christian morals and in the second from the adultery associated with chivalric love. The Latin elegies in particular render the old frank pagan view of love which is to be found in much seventeenth-century English poetry – in Donne, Herrick, Carew, Suckling and many others – though in Milton there is none of the libertinism of these 'courtly' poets. *Paradise Lost* also contains some of the most passionate and moving love poetry in the language.

One such passage is almost too well known to quote, but setting it in this context may reveal its tenderness. It is Eve speaking to Adam:

> With thee conversing I forget all time,
> All seasons and thir change, all please alike.
> Sweet is the breath of morn, her rising sweet,
> With charm of earliest Birds; pleasant the Sun
> When first on this delightful Land he spreads
> His orient Beams, on herb, tree, fruit, and flowr,
> Glistring with dew; fragrant the fertil earth
> After soft showers; and sweet the coming on
> Of grateful Ev'ning mild, then silent Night
> With this her solemn Bird and this fair Moon,
> And these the Gemms of Heav'n, her starrie train:
> But neither breath of Morn when she ascends
> With charm of earliest Birds, nor rising Sun
> On this delightful land, nor herb, fruit, flowr,
> Glistring with dew, nor fragrance after showers,
> Nor grateful Ev'ning mild, nor silent Night
> With this her solemn Bird, nor walk by Moon,
> Or glittering Starr-light without thee is sweet.
>
> [iv. 639–56

Where is there a lovelier love poem?

What some may find a surprising proof that Milton's attitude to love in *Paradise Lost* was as sensual in the old pagan way as that expressed in his early love poems is a line near to those just quoted:

And sweet reluctant amorous delay.

This translates a line in a passage from Ovid's *Ars Amatoria* usually left by translators of that poem in the decent obscurity of a learned tongue:

Sed sensim tarda prolicienda mora (*Ars Amatoria,* ii.718). Milton insists that the love of Adam and Eve in Paradise is both normal and innocent; and he goes on at once to distinguish it from the guilty shame of fallen man, using the word 'honor' to suggest the lasciviousness of 'courtly' love. The distinction of love and lust is at the centre of his treatment of the Fall; but this quotation from Ovid is meant to show unmistakably his view that physical love is an essential and inseparable element in human love at its best.

Milton's views on married love are to be found clearly stated in the *Doctrine and Discipline of Divorce*, the relation of which to his first marriage I have touched on in my first chapter. No doubt Mary's desertion was the immediate occasion of his publishing his views on this subject a year later; but divorce was a much debated question in Protestant countries at this time and Milton had interested himself in it since the Horton days, as is shown by entries in his *Commonplace Book*. He was discussing a question much in the minds of all reformers; and though his views are characteristically bold and unorthodox he handles it as a public not as a private question. His main theme is that to grant divorce, as was the law then, only for adultery is to degrade the whole idea and purpose of marriage, in which intellectual and spiritual companionship should be the first consideration. Accordingly he advocates the granting of divorce on application to those who find themselves unsuited to each other in mind or character, or for what today is called incompatibility of temperament. It was not that he held Hollywood views but that he thought of marriage as 'the marriage of true minds', and as the relief for man's solitariness rather than his merely fleshly desires. He quotes Genesis: 'It is not good that man should be alone; I will make him a help meet for him.' 'A meet and happy conversation', he comments, 'is the chiefest and noblest end of mariage.' If there proves to be an 'indisposition, unfitness or contrariety of mind, . . . hindring and ever likely to hinder the main benefits of conjugall society, which are solace and peace', it is better the pair should part than make a vain attempt 'to fadge together and combine as they may, to their unspeakable

[58]

wearisomness and despaire of all sociable delight in the ordinance that God establisht to that very end.'

He recurs again and again to his principal point that marriage is not meant only or chiefly for relief of that 'other burning of lust'. 'St. *Paul* saith, *It is better to marry then to burn* . . . : but what might this burning mean? Certainly not the meer motion of carnall lust, not the meer goad of a sensitive desire; God does not principally take care for such cattell. What is it then but that desire which God put into *Adam* in Paradise before he knew the sin of incontinence . . . the desire and longing to put off an unkindly solitarines by uniting another body, but not without a fit soule to his in the cheerfull society of wedlock. . . . this pure and inbred desire of joyning to it selfe in conjugall fellowship a pure conversing soul (which desire is properly call'd love) which is *stronger then death,* as the spouse of Christ thought, *many waters cannot quench it, neither can the floods drown it* . . . for if there be not a more human burning which mariage must satisfie, or els may be dissolv'd, then that of copulation, mariage cannot be honorable for the meet reducing and terminating of lust between two: seeing many beasts in voluntary and chosen couples, live altogether as unadulterously, and are as truly maried in that respect.' This contains the substance of the dialogue on wedded love between Raphael and Adam in Book VIII of *Paradise Lost.*

Milton looks at the problem of divorce mainly from the man's point of view, which shows him more modest than those men who pretend to speak for women. He assumes man's superiority over women: 'Who can be ignorant that woman was created for man, and not man for woman?' This was the universal view then, not one peculiar to Milton. It is important in connexion with *Paradise Lost* to realize that the belief in man's superiority was accepted dogma, confirmed by Scripture, and expressed by none more firmly than the amorist poets of the time. Milton's conception of marriage is however more honourable to women than that of most people of the period. His argument implies that woman is capable of being a true companion to man in every way, even intellectually. If man's domination is taken for granted he allows, in *Tetrachordon*, that 'it is no small glory to him, that a creature so like him, should be made subject to him'; and he is willing to recognize exceptionally cases where the husband may admit his wife's superiority (even though this is deplorable) 'if she exceed her husband in prudence and dexterity, and he contentedly yeeld, for then a superior and more natural law comes in, that the wiser should govern the less wise, whether male or female.' And, although he considers it the man's responsibility to determine the question of divorce, he thinks it better if the parting is by mutual consent.

That Milton's views on the relation of the sexes corresponded to those universally held could be illustrated from any writer of the time on the subject, so I content myself with quoting from the marriage service in Edward VI's Second Prayer Book: 'Saint Paul . . . techeth you thus: Ye women submit yourselves unto your husbands as unto the Lord: for the husband is the wives head, even as Christ is the head of the Church . . . let the wives be in subjection unto their husbands in all things.'

Much modern thought on this subject is vitiated by unreality. The feminist movement has certainly demonstrated that woman can be the equal of man in many activities in which she was formerly thought naturally inferior, but nature has set limits to equality on both sides; the differences between the sexes remain. The idea of an absolute equality of the sexes is illogical and contradicted by experience. However harmonious a marriage is, ultimate authority must lie either with the man or the woman; the married state can never be one of equipollence. In the last resort it must be either the man or the woman who rules; and for a well ordered society it must be known and acknowledged which it is. Except in some primitive societies it is the universal law that the man is head of the family. Milton recognizes this fact; and it is of value for us today to have the case fully presented, as it is in *Paradise Lost*.

Chapter 3

DICTION

The diction and rhetoric of *Paradise Lost* is nowadays regarded with disfavour. There are fashions in style as in other things. During the eighteenth century Shakespeare was looked on as an irregular genius and as inferior to Milton as an artist; his language was criticized as careless and incorrect, whilst Milton's was admired as the nearest approach in English to classical clarity, splendour and weight. What the neoclassics especially criticized in Shakespeare was the recurrence of 'low and vulgar language'. This is well illustrated by Johnson's famous criticism of Macbeth's speech before the murder of Duncan, with its 'heav'n peep through the blanket of the dark'. (It is true that Johnson also criticized Milton's language as unnatural, but I shall be returning to that.) With the rise of the Romantic movement the neoclassics and their doctrines fall into disesteem, a taste for the Elizabethans is revived, and Shakespeare's artistry, including his language, comes to be more and more appreciated. Yet Milton still holds his own throughout the nineteenth century and up to the 1914 war. A. E. Housman for instance maintained the older view that, though Shakespeare was the greater genius, Milton was the better artist as a direct result of his training in classical literature. It is well to keep in mind that the style of *Paradise Lost* was thought supremely good by all our principal poets from Dryden to Bridges.

For his style in *Paradise Lost* Milton since 1918 has been used as a whipping-boy by the devotees of the ruling school of

[62]

poetry in our time, a school that has looked to Shakespeare and Donne as its models. The revolt against Milton by T. S. Eliot and his school was one of those recurring revolts in literary history that are necessary to the renewal of health and vigour in poetry; it was a revolt against the dominance of a master who did not help and was felt to hinder the purposes of the new poets. Such revolts tend to exaggerate the features of a style that are reckoned contrary and inimical to the new poetry, and to overlook the features that are common to all good styles. Such errors may be forgiven the poet; it is not however for critics to be camp-followers of the poets in these fighting activities but rather to redress the balance between the old and the new, to sift the facts and to discover how far the differences are differences of emphasis rather than of substance.

In his British Academy lecture of 1947 Eliot told us why he had attacked Milton, as a bad influence, twenty years earlier: 'Milton does, as I have said, represent poetry at the extreme limit from prose; and it was one of our tenets that verse should have the virtues of prose, that diction should become assimilated to cultivated contemporary speech, before aspiring to the elevation of poetry. Another tenet was that the subject-matter and the imagery of poetry should be extended to topics and objects related to the life of a modern man or woman; that we were to seek the non-poetic, to seek even material refractory to transmutation into poetry, and words and phrases which had not been used in poetry before. And the poetry of Milton could be of no help: it was only a hindrance.' Of the relation of Milton's material and imagery to contemporary life, that is Milton's contemporary life, I shall have something to say in Chapter 5; but as to the reason for the attack on Milton's diction, one remembers that Wordsworth, who also led a revolution to bring poetic language back into relation with contemporary speech, accepted Milton as his master.

[63]

In support of this view of Milton's language Eliot quotes Johnson's judgment: 'Throughout all his greater works there prevails an uniform peculiarity of Diction, a mode and cast of expression which bears little resemblance to that of any former writer; and which is so far removed from common use, that an unlearned reader, when he first opens the book, finds himself surprised by a new language . . . but such is the power of his poetry, that his call is obeyed without resistance, the reader feels himself in captivity to a higher and nobler mind, and criticism sinks in admiration.' 'This criticism', comments Eliot, 'seems to me substantially true: indeed, unless we accept it, I do not think we are in the way to appreciate the peculiar greatness of Milton. His style is not a *classic* style, in the sense that it is not the elevation of a *common* style. . . . It is from the foundation, and in every particular, a personal style, not based upon common speech, or common prose, or direct communication of meaning. . . . In Milton there is always the maximal, never the minimal, alteration of ordinary language. Every distortion of construction, the foreign idiom, the use of a word in a foreign way or with the meaning of the word from which it is derived rather than the accepted meaning in English, every idiosyncracy is a particular act of violence which Milton has been the first to commit.' But he concludes in similar vein to Johnson: 'the remoteness of Milton's verse from ordinary speech, his invention of his own poetic language, seems to me one of the marks of his greatness.'

Dr. Johnson and Dr. Eliot agree in a strange paradox: Milton 'writ no language', as Johnson, quoting his namesake, says, and yet he was master of a great compelling poetic style. The paradox starts from a general impression of the style derived from certain facts about it; this impression is then developed into a wholesale description which ignores all the other facts of the case. Eliot's account of Milton's style is what he fancies it ought to be, and what it must be

[64]

to justify his theme, his *apologia*; there is no attempt to check back, to test his argument against the text. It is true that there are some obvious artifices and mannerisms in Milton's style which, taken by themselves, would lead one to suppose it a highly artificial style; but these artifices and mannerisms are not the substance of the style, as Eliot would have us think. There are in particular the Latinisms — the Latin idioms and syntax and word order, and above all the use of words in their Latin senses; these are devices for attaining in English something of the effect of the loaded line of Latin verse, which is a legitimate aim in a poem that deliberately emulates Virgil. But despite these devices it is simply not true that Milton's language is not based on common English, on the current educated speech of his time: how in that case could it be an effective, let alone a great English poetic style? If it is not English, plain English, that he writes, he has failed in his purpose of inventing an English epic style in imitation of Homer and Virgil; it can be no more than a misguided, freakish experiment, which is just what it appears to be in Eliot's description of it. It is true that his language is original, as that of all good poets is: it is not true that it is idiosyncratic, or a perpetual distortion of current idiom. And it is not true that Milton was the first to use the various Latinisms objected to; the first to use them systematically were the seventeenth-century translators of Latin poetry, such as Sandys in his verse translation of Ovid. Milton, with his stronger command of language, only did it better, more convincingly. And because of his command of language, the foreign elements in his diction do not make his poetry more difficult to understand than original poetry normally is; indeed, it is in the main an unusually clear and forceful style. Eliot compares *Paradise Lost* to *Finnegans Wake*, being both 'by blind musicians'; but anyone attempting to read the latter for the first time, unaided, will be continually or completely baffled, whereas a schoolboy coming to *Paradise Lost* for the first time, as I myself can testify, may read on uninterruptedly, hardly noticing difficulties of diction or syntax.

But these general arguments about a technical question get us nowhere. The only way of settling this question of Milton's language is to examine it in some detail, and of course in relation to the English of his time. I shall attempt to do this in regard to the main criticisms that have been brought against it. First, there is the objection to his generalized descriptions, his preference of abstract to concrete words. This habit is said to be due to his weak visual imagination, which Eliot attributes to his weak eyesight and subsequent blindness; I shall have occasion to question this theory later. For the moment it can be admitted that his descriptions are more often generic than particular, at least in the scenes in Heaven and Hell. In such descriptions he does not prompt the imagination by selected detail to realize an individual figure or scene; he concentrates rather on the general impression itself. The reason is that the figures and scenes in these parts of the poem are themselves of representative rather than of singular interest; to individualize them would be to destroy the effect aimed at. A good example of this generic description occurs in the characterisation of Belial:

> In Courts and Palaces he also Reigns
> And in luxurious Cities, where the noise
> Of riot ascends above thir loftiest Towrs,
> And injury and outrage: And when Night
> Darkens the Streets, then wander forth the Sons
> Of *Belial*, flown with insolence and wine. [i. 497–502

Most of the key words here are general or abstract nouns. The picture presented is distinct and forcible, and it is probable that the poet was recording his personal experience of Restoration London; but it is required that the scene should convey a general not a local conception. Such substitution of abstract for concrete words to render physical appearances is frequent in the relation of events in Heaven and Hell. Milton thereby attains an effect of immeasurable grandeur, diffuses a sense of the infinite through a finite form:

> And with the Majesty of darkness round
> Covers his Throne.   [ii. 266–7

The same method is used in the description of persons as of scenes, as in this characterization of Beëlzebub:

>   deep on his Front engraven
> Deliberation sat and public care;
> And Princely counsel in his face yet shon,
> Majestic though in ruin.   [ii. 302–5

The use of an adjective for a noun is a similar device, describing physical appearances by qualities: 'the palpable obscure', 'the vast abrupt'.

There was one chief reason why Milton was able to avail himself of the grandeur of abstract words without his style becoming grandiose: he had a scholar's sense of the substance, the concrete imagery and wealth of associated meaning stored in these words. A good example is when Mammon, speaking of what they can do to render their new abode more habitable and agreeable, says,

> Nor want we skill or art, from whence to raise
> Magnificence.   [ii. 272–3

The one word 'magnificence' renders completely the idea of inventive and constructive activity, and brings in its train a host of physical images, of palatial and costly buildings, all the pomp and circumstance of civilization. How much the imaginative effect of these scenes and figures in *Paradise Lost* depends on this kind of diction can be tested by comparing the powerful impression produced in reading with

c   [67]

the vague notions one can summon up afterwards. One has for instance no precise idea of Milton's Chaos (it would be wrong if one had), yet while reading the latter part of Book II the imagination is held and satisfied by the vigour of the description. As Hazlitt says in *On Shakespeare and Milton*, Milton perhaps 'stimulates us more in the reading, and less afterwards'. He dominates our minds by the sheer power of words. It is partly by the power of words that he creates the illusion of scenes and figures outside the scope of human experience; his other chief means, as we shall see, is the simile. One cannot object to such diction as a fault unless one first objects to the subject-matter that made it necessary. When Milton's grand style fails, as occasionally it does, the failure is due not to the diction but to the want of invention, as in these lines from the otherwise wonderful description of Death:

> black it stood as Night,
> Fierce as ten Furies, terrible as Hell,
> And shook a dreadful Dart.   [ii. 670–2

This tells the imagination no more about Death than that he was terrible and threatened Satan with his spear. For once Milton is grandiose.

Turning next to the Latinisms in *Paradise Lost* it is worth noting first that certain Latinisms, which one might expect to find there because they are prominent in eighteenth-century neoclassical verse, do not in fact occur. One is the joining of a concrete descriptive epithet to an abstract noun, as in 'fleecy care'. This is a device for attaining the compression of Latin verse. A similar device is the joining of a concrete descriptive epithet to a collective noun, as in 'the feathery or the footed game'. The one instance, I think, in Milton is 'finny drove' in *Comus*, 115, which is taken from Spenser and is applied to a shoal of fish seen in the moonlight; it is a very effective phrase – as Geoffrey Tillotson has said, 'he wanted the reader to be aware of an exquisite battery of fins'. Such expressions in *Paradise Lost* as 'Angelical and Human kind', or 'brutal kind' for 'beasts', do not fall into this category, since they lack the picturesque detail and are a normal form of speech; there is for instance Shakespeare's 'mortal kind'. Yet another feature of neo-classical diction in which Milton does not indulge is the periphrastic descriptive phrase in place of the common name for an everyday object: 'glaz'd optic tube' for 'telescope' may seem to be such a periphrasis, but the fact is that 'optic tube' or 'optic glass' were the familiar English terms, 'tele-scope' the more foreign and pedantic; up to at least the middle of the seventeenth century 'telescope' keeps its Latin or Italian form.

Of the Latinisms that do occur I shall deal first with words used in their original Latin instead of their English senses. The most important point about these words in *Paradise Lost* is that most of them were current in educated speech of the Elizabethan and Stuart periods, when all literate people were versed in Latin; they were as natural to English lips and as much a part of the living language as Anglo-Saxon words. They are foreign to the modern reader only because these meanings have been submerged. It is rarely that Milton can be suspected of being idiosyncratic in these usages. Two instances from *Paradise Lost* in which he may be idiosyncratic, and which have not, I think, been previously noted, will illustrate the expressive value he gets from this resource of language. One is the use of 'humid' in

> where Rivers now
> Stream, and perpetual draw thir humid train.
> [vii. 305–6

'humid' is here used not in its primary Latin sense of 'wet' but in its secondary Latin sense, 'liquid, flowing'. The reader certainly needs to be alert for such occasions, if the poetry is

[69]

not to be spoilt; but then he should be warned by the fact
that 'wet train' is flat and ridiculous. The other instance will
take longer to deal with. It is the use of 'shade' for 'tree', in
which Milton is only idiosyncratic in his fondness for it. The
word occurs sixty times in his poetry, and two out of three
times as a metonymy for tree, bush, woods or foliage. This is
an imitation of 'umbra' for 'arbor' in Latin poetic usage, as
in Virgil's

> Spargite humum foliis, inducite fontibus umbras.
> [*Ecl.*, v. 40

which the Connington-Nettleship note translates, 'Sow the
turf with flowers and plant trees (overshadowing) the spring.'
That Milton was not alone in adopting this Latinism is
shown by Crashaw's use of it in his translation of the
Georgics, ii.324–45, in the verses entitled *Out of Virgil, In
the Praise of Spring:*

> no lone shade, but rings
> With chatting Birds delicious murmurings,

where 'lone shade' renders Virgil's 'avia . . . virgulta'
('pathless thickets'). Milton's continual use of the word in
this sense throughout his poetry, from *Il Penseroso* to
Paradise Regain'd, suggests that visually trees appealed to
him especially for their shadowing foliage. I hope no one
will say or think that this was due to his shortsightedness: in
Comus 'crisped shades' presents the shapes both of the leaves
and their sharp sunlit shadows. Some examples from
Paradise Lost will illustrate the various applications of the
word. It naturally occurs most frequently in the descriptions
of Paradise in Book IV. Paradise, as Satan approaches it
through Eden, is seen as a sylvan citadel, its 'verdurous
wall' crowning a high cliff of trees:

> and over head up grew
> Insuperable highth of loftiest shade,

Cedar and Pine and Firr and branching **Palm**,
A Silvan Scene, and as the ranks ascend
Shade above shade, a woodie Theatre
Of stateliest view.   [iv. 137–42

In the description of Adam's bower 'shade' means 'shading foliage':

                    the roofe
Of thickest covert was inwoven shade
Laurel and Mirtle, and what higher grew
Of firm and fragrant leaf.   [iv. 692–5

'Laurel and Mirtle' is in apposition to 'shade'. A particularly clear example is at iv.325–7:

Under a tuft of shade that on a green
Stood whispering soft, by a fresh Fountain side
They sat them down.

'tuft' means 'clump (of trees)'; Shakespeare has 'tuft of Olives', 'tuft of Pines', 'tuft of trees'. A shade, in the ordinary sense, it may be noticed, does not whisper. Uriel tells how from his station in the sun he watched Satan after he had alighted on earth:

Mine eye persu'd him still, but under shade
Lost sight of him.   [iv. 572–3

The only comment, so far as I know, on 'under shade' is Jonathan Richardson's, 'Satan hid himself in Darkness', which means, presumably, that he assumed a magic cloak of invisibility, for it was broad day; but there is no suggestion here or elsewhere that Satan so hid himself. What he does, as we have been told previously in lines 134 seq., is to enter the thicket on the lowest slopes of the mount of Paradise. Two examples from other parts of the poem will suffice. The Serpent, waiting in ambush for Eve,

hid among sweet Flowrs and Shades.   [ix. 408

Here 'shades' clearly means 'bushes'. Finally, there is Eve's lament on being told of the expulsion from Paradise:

> Must I leave thee Paradise? thus leave
> Thee Native Soil, these happie Walks and Shades,
> Fit haunt of Gods? [xi. 269–71

There is no poetic sense to be made of these and other places unless one takes 'shade' in its Virgilian sense. It is strange that this sense should not have been noted in commentaries or in the *O.E.D.*

But most of the words used by Milton in their Latin senses were, as I have said, current English of the time. The difficulty for the modern reader is that many of them have remained common words but have lost these Latin meanings. Any strangeness or remoteness in Milton's language is due for the most part, as with all older authors, to such alterations in the meanings of words. Again, there are comparatively few obsolete words in Milton, no more than in any other writer whose vocabulary has been kept alive by his being continually read; 'jocond' for instance is now an exclusively literary word, obsolete in the sense that it would never be used now by a writer or speaker, but it was not so when used by Chaucer, Wycliffe, Shakespeare and Milton, and a modern reader knows it from them. In any case obsolete words are at once recognizable as such and will be looked up, if necessary, in a glossary. It is the obsolete meanings of words still in general use that puzzle or mislead. When for instance God addresses the Son with the words, 'O thou my sole complacence!' it sounds oddly smug unless one knows that the word, as in the Latin, was then used not only of self-satisfaction but applied generally to satisfaction or pleasure in other persons and things; as in Jeremy Taylor's 'spiritual comforts and complacencies'. Milton's use of 'obvious' in its various Latin senses is often cited as an example of his un-English diction: (1) 'standing in the way, confronting' ('obvious hill', 'obvious breast'); (2) 'open, liable (to)' ('obvious to dispute'); (3) 'ready, forthcoming' ('obvious duty', 'not obvious, not obtrusive, not retir'd'). Yet these three uses are all to be found in such Elizabethan writers as William Webbe, Drayton and 'well-languaged' Daniel; and they are all older than the modern, more general and therefore duller meaning, 'plain, manifest'. Many of Milton's Latin usages are found in Shakespeare: 'apparent' ('visible'), 'secure' ('over-confident'), 'prevent' ('anticipate': the first quotation under the modern sense in *O.E.D.* is dated 1663). 'Combustion' in the Latin sense of 'utter confusion, destruction' occurs in Shakespeare:

> And prophesying with accents terrible
> Of dire combustion and confus'd events.
> [*Macb.* II. iii. 63–64

which corresponds to Milton's

> With hideous ruin and combustion down
> To bottomless perdition.   [i. 46–47

It has often been remarked that many of Milton's Latinistic words do double service by reinforcing the English sense by the original meaning; this has expressive value whether the word be of foreign or native origin, and it serves Milton's aim of approximating to the Latin density of style. The fallen angels are 'abject' ('cast down') and 'afflicted' ('struck down') both literally and figuratively. 'reluctant' is used thrice in the poem, each time with the literal Latin sense ('struggling' or 'struggling against') alongside the modern English sense:

> and smoke to roul
> In duskie wreathes, reluctant flames.   [vi. 57–58

> down he fell
> A monstrous Serpent on his belly prone,
> Reluctant.   [x. 513–15

And sweet reluctant amorous delay.   [iv. 311

Milton's consciousness of the history of words enables
him to revive their original, often concrete, significance, and
so to use them in new contexts. He shows this same skill in
his handling of native words. Compare with 'reluctant
flames' the expression 'bickering flame' ('skirmishing,
wrangling') in the description of the Son's chariot going
into battle:

> And from about him fierce Effusion rould
> Of smoke and bickering flame, and sparkles dire.
>   [vi. 765–6

O.E.D. quotes this as the first use of 'bickering' in the
sense of 'coruscating, flashing, quivering', but this, I think,
is a mistake; the next quotation in the *O.E.D.* under this
sense is from Beckford's *Vathek* (1786), and this looks like
Beckford's misinterpretation of Milton's use. In his prose
Milton always uses the noun in the normal sense of a
skirmish or wrangle as opposed to a set battle: 'onely to turne
his [sc. Charles I] slashing at the Court Gate, to slaughtering
in the Field; his disorderly bickering to an orderly invading.'
(*Eikonoklastes*, Col. ed., V. 114). *Paradise Lost*, like Milton's
early poetry, is not without the refreshment of such homely
words. The word 'charm', for instance, in 'charm of earliest
Birds' (iv. 642) has been confused by some with its
homophone from Latin 'carmen' ('song, incantation'); it is
in fact from the Anglo-Saxon 'cierm' ('clamour' of battle,
etc.'), which had come to be used specifically of the confused
noise of children's and bird's voices, and is still so used in
country districts. It is the unique word for the chatter and
singing of birds at dawn. '*yeanling* Kids' (iii. 434) is another
of what Helen Darbishire calls his 'country words'.

Milton's sonorous Latin words are habitually accom-
panied by simple native words:

> so thick bestrown
> Abject and lost lay these,

is characteristic: 'dark opprobrious den', 'to perplex and dash Maturest Counsels', 'foul exorbitant desires'. (One notes again the Shakespearian cast of these phrases.) 'Sciential sap' (used of the Tree of Knowledge) illustrates not only this point but the resources of expression supplied by Milton's learning; there is no other single word for 'producing knowledge' than 'sciential'. It will be noticed that this mingling of native and Latin words results in the interplay of monosyllable and polysyllable, giving one of the most effective and satisfying rhythms in English; as in Shakespeare's 'multitudinous seas incarnadine', Thomas Browne's 'diuturnity is a dream and folly of expectation', Wordsworth's 'incommunicable sleep', Matthew Arnold's 'inviolable shade' or Eliot's 'with inviolable voice'. The rhythm is so frequent in Milton as almost to become a mannerism: 'uninterrupted joy, unrivald love', 'unextinguishable fire', 'dark illimitable ocean', 'with indefatigable wings', 'with Frie innumerable swarm'.

Another characteristic of Milton's language is the use of technical terms – military, nautical, sporting, architectural, musical, biological, astronomical, mineralogical, metallurgical – involving a knowledge of all the arts and sciences with which an educated man was then expected to be familiar. These technical terms are also among his words of common usage though many are now obsolete or unfamiliar to the general reader; consequently Milton's exact use of them is not always appreciated. A good example is the passage describing how the devils, under Mammon's direction, perform three distinct industrial operations in getting and working the metal for the building of Pandaemonium: one gang mines the ore (only gold is named but other metals are implied in the account); a second gang smelts the crude

[75]

ore to extract the metal and refine it; a third gang founds or casts the metal. It is an elaborate poetical description, firmly based on exact knowledge of the industrial processes involved. I quote from the second edition, noting one important emendation:

> There stood a Hill not far whose griesly top
> Belch'd fire and rowling smoak; the rest entire
> Shon with a glossie scurff, undoubted sign
> That in his womb was hid metallic Ore,
> The work of Sulphur. . . . Soon had his crew
> Op'nd into the Hill a spacious wound
> And dig'd out ribs of Gold. . . .
> Nigh on the Plain in many cells prepar'd,
> That underneath had veins of liquid fire
> Sluc'd from the Lake, a second multitude
> With wondrous Art found out the massie Ore,
> Severing each kind, and scum'd the Bullion dross:
> A third as soon had form'd within the ground
> A various mould, and from the boyling cells
> By strange conveyance fill'd each hollow nook, . . .
> 　　　　　　　　　　　　　　　　　　[i. 670–707

703 found out *Ed. 2*: founded *MS., Ed. I*

Bentley called *found out* 'a vile Fault . . . instead of *Founded*, melted'; and other editors have agreed with him. To 'found', however, does not mean to melt but to pour the molten metal into moulds, which is the operation performed by the third gang. By some accident the technical term 'founded' was originally misapplied to the second of the operations, and that is why Milton changed it to 'found out', i.e. 'discovered or obtained (what was hidden)'. That Milton knew just what he was talking about is proved by his accurate use of technical terms throughout the passage. The information may be found in Agricola's *De Re Metallica*, the textbook on mining and metallurgy for nearly 200 years after its publication in 1556; for an English version of the processes

[76]

and technical terms there is Sir John Pettus's *Fleta Minor* (London, 1686). Here are the technical terms used by Milton: 'metallic Ore' is the gross ore as it is dug out of the ground, a compound of metalliferous and of non-metalliferous minerals such as earth and rock; 'ribs' are 'veins' of metal in rock, so that 'ribs of Gold' are 'reef' as distinct from 'alluvial' gold; 'massie Ore' is the metal extracted from the gross ore by smelting; 'Severing each kind' describes the separation of the different metals; 'scum'd the Bullion dross' describes the refining of the metal; 'mould' is the form or matrix in which the metal is cast. All these are technical terms correctly used, and there seems to me no doubt therefore that 'found out' is also the correct reading.

Before leaving this topic of the various elements in Milton's diction I will illustrate their relative proportions in a continuous passage. I take for the purpose part of the description of the creation of fish and birds in Book VII. Although the general meaning is clear enough, no less than fourteen words in these ten lines would need glossing in a modern edition. Of these three are Latinisms, two are technical terms, one is a nonce-use, one a now archaic participle; the remaining seven are everyday words used in senses now obsolete, all of which occur in Shakespeare.

> Or in thir Pearlie shells at ease, attend
> Moist nutriment, or under Rocks thir food
> In jointed Armour watch: on smooth the Seal
> And bended Dolphins play: . . . .
> Mean while the tepid Caves, and Fens and shores
> Thir Brood as numerous hatch, from th' Egg that soon
> Bursting with kindly rupture forth disclos'd
> Thir callow young, but featherd soon and fledge
> They summd thir Penns, and soaring th' air sublime
> With clang despis'd the ground, under a cloud
> In prospect.   [vii. 407–23

Here are the glosses and Shakespeare references: *attend*, 'await', cf. *M.W.W*, I. i. 281, 'dinner attends you'; *watch*, 'watch for', cf. 2*H. VI*, II. iv. 7; *smooth*, 'stretch of calm water in rough seas', nautical; *Dolphins*, 'porpoises', cf. *Tw. N*, I. ii. 15; *kindly*, 'natural', cf. *T. of A.*, II. ii. 226; *rupture*, 'bursting, breaking', cf. *Per*, II. i. 167, 'rupture of the sea'; *disclos'd*, 'hatched', cf. *Ham.*, III. i. 174, 'the hatch and the disclose'; *fledge*, 'fledged', form of the past participle in use until the eighteenth century; *summd*, 'completed', generally used in this sense but, according to *O.E.D.*, a nonce-word as used of birds' feathers; *Penns*, 'flight feathers', technical term; *sublime*, 'on high', a not unusual Latinism; *clang*, 'scream of large birds', again a common Latinism; *despis'd*, 'looked down on,' literally, Latinism; *prospect*, 'appearance', cf. *Oth.*, III. iii. 399.

Enough has been said to show that Milton's diction is composed of various elements, and to indicate that the basis is the common educated speech of the time. It remains to consider the objection that his syntax and word order are Latinistic and foreign. This will lead on to the larger question of style as distinct from diction. The syntax of *Paradise Lost* is certainly highly organized, and to some extent on the pattern of Latin poetry; but the number of Latin and other foreign constructions has been exaggerated. What Milton aims at is the economy and density of Latin expression. This is seen in such a line, not peculiarly Latin in construction, as

Go; for thy stay, not free, absents thee more. [ix. 372

Helen Darbishire likens this sentence to 'a piece of action, or a scene in drama in which each word is an actor standing in direct and dynamic relation with its fellows. There are no supers. The result is that the word has its power raised to the highest.' It is however in the long sentences, so frequent in the poem, that we clearly see Milton's use of

[78]

Latin syntax. The prime necessity in a long sentence is logical development, and this is the chief characteristic of Milton's epic style. It is finely articulated. His manipulation of a succession of subordinate clauses, participial and appositional phrases, and the deft placing of words, owe much to his Latin models, but they are not un-English; nor is the occasional ablative absolute. At any rate they are the chief means of keeping these long intricate sentences on course. The exact placing of these clauses and phrases, often without connectives, builds a structure as firm and balanced as a drystone wall. Take Satan's speech on his return to Hell:

> Thrones, Dominations, Princedoms, Vertues, Powers,
> For in possession such, not onely of right,
> I call ye and declare ye now, returnd
> Successful beyond hope, to lead ye forth
> Triumphant out of this infernal Pit
> Abominable, accurst, the house of wo,
> And Dungeon of our Tyrant: Now possess,
> As Lords, a spacious World, to our native Heaven
> Little inferior, by my adventure hard
> With peril great achiev'd.   [x. 460–9

And he goes on to relate in some thirty lines, equally succinctly and clearly, the complete story of his venture. The lines quoted are a typical passage, moving straight on through the complicated grammatical structure, using only two conjunctions but relying on the ordering of the words and the continuity of meaning; and there is no 'distortion of construction'.

In the ordering of his single words one again sees the effect of Milton's study and practise of Latin verse. The Latin poet, writing in an inflected language, could distribute his words in varying order, and so could develop the sense flexibly, organically, and in a cumulative way; this latitude in the placing of his words also made it easier to control the stresses and movement of the verse in accordance with the meaning. In English, where the order of the words is more determinate of the sense, such distribution of the words is obviously restricted; but Milton goes as far as possible in reproducing this cumulative style and this responsive movement of the verse. He will reverse the normal order of subject and verb, and separate a verb from its component adverb: 'Now came still Ev'ning on'. He will place an epithet after its noun in order to emphasize it:

> adventure hard
> With peril great achiev'd.

He will flank a noun with epithets fore and aft. With reference to this Hazlitt remarks that 'Milton has great gusto; he repeats his blow twice.' And he instances

> where *Chineses* drive
> With Sails and Wind thir canie Waggons light.
>
> [iii. 438–9

The second epithet 'light' would lose all its force if it did not come after 'Waggons', as a follow-up. Landor observed that Milton probably adopted this device from Italian verse, where it is frequent. A variation on this method of distributing the weight of his epithets is that of following epithet and noun in the normal order with noun and epithet in reverse order:

> Of unoriginal *Night* and *Chaos* wild.   [x. 477
> Innumerable force of Spirits armd.   [i. 101

These are simple enough devices but they are used skilfully to vary the texture of the verse. I cannot think that an unprejudiced reader dislikes them or finds them, familiar as they are in our older verse, either foreign or difficult.

But what of the style in general, resulting from these various elements of diction and syntax? In examining particular features of Milton's style it is easy to give a false idea of its general character. Thus the impression conveyed by

some discussions of this topic is that *Paradise Lost* is written
in an unvaryingly elevated and exotic style, entirely in the
grand manner; whereas on the contrary the style is constantly changing in answer to the needs of the narrative,
to its subject-matter and moods. Pope pointed out that there
are different levels of style in the poem, which we may call
high, middle and low. 'Milton', says Pope, 'is not lavish of his
exotic words and phrases everywhere alike, but employs
them much more when the subject is marvellous and strange
as in the scenes in Heaven and Hell, than where it is turned
to the natural and agreeable as in the pictures of Paradise.
In the lower sort of narration the character of the style is
simplicity and purity.' Since he distinguishes the scenes in
Heaven and Hell from those in Paradise it would seem that
by 'the lower sort of narration' Pope meant the scenes between Adam and Eve after the Fall. And it is true that here,
as one would expect, the language does become more simple
and direct. There are Eve's words after her fall and before
Adam's:

> So dear I love him, that with him all deaths
> I could endure, without him live no life.   [ix. 832–3

Or when seeking reconciliation with Adam:

> While yet we live, scarce one short hour perhaps,
> Between us two let there be peace.   [x. 923–4

And Adam, after God has heard his prayer for forgiveness:

> peace returnd
> Home to my brest.   [xi. 153–4

But though there is general truth in Pope's distinction, in
the sense that there is a predominant style in each of these
different sections of the poem, his statement is misleading if
taken to mean more than it says, if taken to mean that there
is no variation in the predominant styles in these different

parts. The pure and simple style for instance occurs in every Book, and notably at the crucial moments in the story. At the start of Satan's decisive speech in the debate in Hell:

> long is the way
> And hard, that out of Hell leads up to light.
> [ii. 432–3

When about to take off into Chaos:

> Into this wild Abyss the warie Fiend
> Stood on the brink of Hell and lookd a while,
> Pondering his Voyage; for no narrow frith
> He had to cross. [ii. 917–20

And again at the close of his triumphant speech on his return to Hell:

> What remains, ye Gods,
> But up and enter now into full bliss. [x. 502–3

When God asks who will pay the sacrifice for man's salvation:

> Dwells in all Heaven charitie so dear?
> He askd, but all the Heav'nly Quire stood mute,
> And silence was in Heav'n. [iii. 216–18

The Son going into battle:

> He onward came, farr off his coming shon, ... [vi. 768

The Son calming Chaos:

> Silence, ye troubl'd waves, and thou Deep, peace, ...
> [vii. 216

Adam comforting Eve after her evil dream:

> So cheerd he his fair Spouse, and she was cheerd,
> But silently a gentle tear let fall

From either eye, and wip'd them with her hair.

[v. 129–31

The turning point in Satan's temptation of Eve:

Into the Heart of *Eve* his words made way.   [ix. 550

and

To whom the wilie adder, blithe and glad.   [ix. 625

Such brief quotations may be held to prove only that Milton knew how to use simple language on occasion; and this too may be regarded as only another facet of his conscious art. The supreme test of the writer, however, is the ability to write naturally, without mannerism or artifice, using the best words, whether simple or not, in the best order. That Milton commands such a style could be illustrated from every part of the poem. I will take a passage from Belial's speech in the debate in Pandaemonium, advising against Moloch's counsel to wreak their revenge on Heaven by armed assault, even though it should entail another repulse and perhaps their utter extinction:

Thus repulst, our final hope
Is flat despair: we must exasperate
Th' Almighty Victor to spend all his rage,
And that must end us, that must be our cure,
To be no more; sad cure; for who would lose,
Though full of pain, this intellectual being,
Those thoughts that wander through Eternity,
To perish rather, swallowd up and lost
In the wide womb of uncreated night,
Devoid of sense and motion?

[ii. 142–54

This reminds one of Wordsworth at his best. Such writing does not date, for it expresses a universal thought in common but exciting language. It is a perfect example of what Eliot explicitly denies to Milton, a classic

[83]

style. It is of such writing that Eliot can say, it is 'a personal style, not based upon common speech, or common prose, or direct communication of meaning.' One wonders then where this *O Altitudo* of style is to be found.

I shall attempt no analysis of the verse of *Paradise Lost*, but content myself with remarking that there is the same variety in the versification as in the language. The verse adapts itself to heroic or domestic action, to description, exposition, oratory and talk, and to lyricism, with a flexibility that has not been equalled in English heroic poetry. The last proof of its range and versatility is the lyrical passages, which might have been thought beyond the measure of blank verse, especially a blank verse so girded as Milton's. A leading anti-Miltonist is reported to have said that *Paradise Lost* was the one book he took into the trenches in France in the 1914 war because it was the only verse that could stand up to the hammering of the guns. Evidently his ear was different from Landor's: 'After I have been reading the *Paradise Lost*, I can take up no other poet with satisfaction. I seem to have left the music of Handel for the music of the streets, or at best for drums and fifes. . . . In our English heroic verse, such as Milton has composed it, there is a much greater variety of feet, of movement, of musical notes and bars, than in the Greek heroic; and the final sounds are incomparably more diversified. . . . Averse as I am to every thing relating to theology, and especially to the view of it thrown open by this poem, I recur to it incessantly as the noblest specimen in the world of eloquence, harmony, and genius.'

Chapter 4

THE FUNCTION
OF THE EPIC SIMILE

The accepted view of the function of the epic similes in
Paradise Lost is indicated by the epithets applied to them —
longtailed, decorative, digressive, detached. This view
derives from the neoclassical period. Towards the end of
the seventeenth century the epic or Homeric simile became
a distinct topic of controversy, arising out of the general
controversy known as the Quarrel of the Ancients and
Moderns. This, like all wide controversies, was full of confusing cross-currents, but in general we may say that the
Moderns were those who maintained the superiority of
modern over ancient literature, not only because it is more
entertaining to the modern mind but because it observed
more strictly the neoclassical rules deduced from the theory
and practice of the ancient writers. The Moderns in short
were, as W. P. Ker said, 'more correct than the Ancients,
more classical than Homer'. They, in their own opinion,
were the true neoclassics. The question at issue had been
inherent in the literary situation since the Revival of Learning but the historical Quarrel started in the French Academy
between Charles Perrault and Nicolas Boileau in the last
decade of the seventeenth century, after Perrault had stated
the case of the Moderns in its most extreme and provocative
form. Between 1688 and 1696 Perrault published the four
volumes of his *Parallèle des anciens et des modernes,* in which
he sought to show that the Moderns excelled the Ancients

in all the arts and sciences, and not least in literature; in the part dealing with poetry he repeatedly censured the admired classical poets, and held up Homer and Pindar in particular as shocking examples of licence and as offenders against the neoclassical rules and standards of taste. Boileau replied to these strictures on the ancient poets in 1698 in *Les Réflexions Critiques,* added to his third edition of his translation of Longinus, dealing particularly in *Réflexion* VI with Perrault's ridicule of what he called Homer's 'comparaison à longue queue'.

It was no accident that Boileau's defence appeared in a translation of and commentary on Longinus; for it was the treatise *On the Sublime,* with its exaltation of the imagination, that provided neoclassical critics with a way of escape, however illogical, from the net of their own dogmas – not only from the dogma of 'correctness' but from the more radical dogma that the imagination is inferior to the reason in poetry. The distinction between the mental faculty referred to indifferently as the 'imagination' or 'fancy' (the distinction between the two was first made by Coleridge), and the faculty variously referred to as the 'reason', 'understanding' or 'judgment', was the basis of neoclassical theory. It can be stated as generally understood by men of letters, without going into philosophical niceties. The imagination or fancy is the faculty whereby we apprehend those images or ideas derived from sense impressions; reason is the faculty whereby we judge those images, or form true ideas corresponding to the underlying reality. Quickness and liveliness of perception, when expressed in words, was called 'wit', which thus became a third synonym for imagination or fancy. Wit was defined in particular as a quickness in seeing similitudes; it is exemplified in what were called 'allusions', a generic term for metaphors, similes and any kind of analogy. The corresponding activity of the reason was in discerning differences. The

[86]

reason scrutinizes ideas in order to identify and distinguish them, and to discern their nature and relations; imagination plays with ideas, inventing phantasms and fictions, or putting one thing for another as in metaphors and similes. It is the function of the reason to investigate the truth of things and to extend knowledge; the imagination is only to be trusted even in its own sphere when working under the control of reason.

These ideas were first applied in English literary criticism by Hobbes in his *Answer to Davenant* (1650), where we find the famous dictum, 'Judgment begets the strength and structure, and Fancy begets the ornaments of a Poem.' These words are not so contemptuous of the imagination as they may seem to a modern reader. 'Ornaments' was a technical term for the 'beauties' of a poem, which included not only imagery, figures of speech and graces of style, but striking ideas and sentiments also. Nevertheless Hobbes's main point is that in both the planning and the execution of a poem, in the choice of words and their sequence no less than in the choice and sequence of incidents, ideas and images, the imagination needs to be under the constant supervision of the reason. Reason is superior in all mental activity, including poetry; it lays the design and directs the execution of a poem as of a prose work. The irrational poetical wit, that fiery Pegasus the imagination, needs always to be restrained by the judgment. Of the innumerable expressions of this view there is none more emphatic than Dryden's in the *Epistle Dedicatory to 'The Rival Ladies'* where he is defending rhyme against blank verse in drama: 'But that benefit I most consider in [rhyme] is, that it bounds and circumscribes the fancy. For imagination in a poet is a faculty so wild and lawless, that like an high-ranging spaniel, it must have clogs tied to it, lest it outrun the judgment.'

Boileau's defence of the longtailed simile was quoted by Addison in the first of his *Spectator* papers on *Paradise Lost,*

[87]

16 February 1712. This is the source of what has ever since been said on the similes of *Paradise Lost*:

'There are also several noble Similes and Allusions in the first Book of *Paradise Lost*. And here I must observe, that when Milton alludes either to Things or Persons, he never quits his Simile till it rises to some very great Idea, which is often foreign to the Occasion that gave Birth to it. The Resemblance does not, perhaps, last above a line or two, but the poet runs on with the Hint, till he has raised out of it some glorious Image or Sentiment, proper to inflame the Mind of the Reader, and to give it that sublime kind of Entertainment, which is suitable to the Nature of an Heroic Poem. Those, who are acquainted with *Homer's* and *Virgil's* way of Writing, cannot but be pleased with this kind of Structure in *Milton's* Similitudes. I am the more particular on this Head, because ignorant Readers, who have formed their Taste upon the quaint Similes, and little Turns of Wit, which are so much in Vogue among Modern Poets, cannot relish these Beauties which are of a much higher nature, and are therefore apt to censure *Milton's* Comparisons, in which they do not see any surprizing Points of Likeness. Monsieur *Perrault* was a Man of this viciated Relish, and for that very Reason has endeavoured to turn into Ridicule several of *Homer's* Similitudes, which he calls *Comparaisons à longue Queue, Long-tail'd Comparisons*. I shall conclude this Paper on the First Book of *Milton* with the Answer which Monsieur *Boileau* makes to Monsieur *Perrault* on this Occasion; "Comparisons, says he, in Odes and Epic Poems are not introduced only to illustrate and embellish the Discourse, but to amuse and relax the Mind of the Reader, by frequently disengaging him from too painful an Attention to the Principal Subject, and by leading him into other agreeable Images. *Homer*, says he, excelled in this Particular, whose Comparisons abound with such Images of Nature as are proper to relieve and diversifie his

[88]

Subjects. . . . To this he adds, as a Maxim universally acknowledged, that it is not necessary in Poetry for the Points of Comparison to correspond with one another exactly, but that a general Resemblance is sufficient, and that too much nicety in this Particular savours of the Rhetorician and Epigrammatist." In short, if we look into the Conduct of *Homer*, *Virgil* and *Milton*, as the great Fable is the Soul of each Poem, so to give their Works an agreeable Variety, their Episodes are so many short Fables, and their Similes so many short Episodes; to which you may add, if you please, that their Metaphors are so many short Similes.'

Here are all the ingredients of the usual comments on the similes of *Paradise Lost*. The similes are expanded beyond the point of the comparison into independent pictures foreign to the occasion; they are excursions of the imagination beyond the needs of the narrative. This was why precisians like Perrault condemned these longtailed similes: the poet's imagination outruns his judgment, resulting in ridiculous impertinences. Yet Addison, like Boileau, will not have this. The digressions are justified, first because they enhance the poetry by glorious images and sentiments; secondly because they supply variety and relief by introducing scenes outside the proper scope of the story; thirdly because a poetical analogy differs from a prosaic or rhetorical one; and finally there is the forced attempt to offer a formal justification by classing these similes with episodes, which were permitted by the neoclassical rules. All this is specious and will not do; it is unprincipled criticism.

The point that a rhetorical differs from a poetical analogy might indeed have been developed into a rational justification, by pointing out that one is directed to persuading the reason and the other the imagination. It is the rhetorical simile that is an illustrative parallel, the success of which depends on the exact correlation of the two things being

[89]

compared; whereas the poetical simile is a symbol, expressing what has to be expressed in a poetical manner. Addison goes a little way towards saying this but stops well short of the clinching statement that these similes justify themselves by imaginative and not by intellectual logic. He is caught in the neoclassical dilemma. He holds that the design and conduct of a poem should be under the direction and control of the reason, and that anything that diverges from the argument or plot, as it could be summarized in prose, is an extravagance of the imagination. These similes of *Paradise Lost* are such extravagances, which he can, however, admire and approve, with the sanction of Longinus, for their imaginative force; but this approval does not follow from his critical premisses, and the most that he can be saying, in reason, is that these similes, in Pope's words, 'overpower criticism, and make us admire even while we disapprove'. He puts up a brave front and praises fervently, but he cannot praise logically.

Other early commentators adopt the same ambiguous attitude. Zachary Pearce for instance, in his *Review of the Text of 'Paradise Lost'* published in 1733 in reply to Bentley's edition, in his note on Book II, 635, echoes Addison: 'Milton in his similitudes, (as is the practice of Homer and Virgil too), after he has shew'd the common resemblance, often takes the liberty of wandring into some unresembling Circumstances; which have no other relation to the Comparison, than that it gave the hint, and (as it were) set fire to the train of his Imagination.' Modern critics have applauded this declaration for the freedom of the imagination, ringing out from a benighted age; but it will not do. On his own critical ground Pearce is crying not for freedom but licence, and for that there can be no critical justification. And after all the neoclassical doctrine was right, that the imagination must be controlled and directed: it is the Aristotelian doctrine that all must subserve the unity of the action, the doctrine Matthew Arnold was to reiterate after the Romantics had had their fling. What put the neoclassics wrong in applying the doctrine was their belief that the principle of control was the same for the imagination as for the reason, and that the working of the imagination and the reason was to be tried by the same criteria. They did not see that the imagination also can reason, that there is a logic of imaginative thinking.

As is well known, a different theory of the imagination was produced by Coleridge and Wordsworth at the end of the eighteenth century. The theory originated with Coleridge, for whom it was not only a literary theory but the principle of a philosophy. Coleridge believed that reality and truth cannot be discovered by dispassionate reasoning but only by an act of the whole mind in which thought and feeling work together, culminating in a direct vision, an intuition of the truth. In March 1801 he writes: 'My opinion is that deep thinking is only attainable by a man of deep feeling; and that all truth is a species of Revelation.' This passionate thinking belongs to the imagination; and he distinguished the imagination in this sense from the fancy. The fancy as defined by him is very much what the eighteenth century understood by poetic wit; while the imagination in his view has the power to create and shape. Thus he described fancy to Crabb Robinson as 'the arbitrary bringing together of things that lie remote'; it 'acts by a sort of juxtaposition'; the imagination 'on the other hand, under excitement, generates and produces a form of its own'. Again in Chapter 13 of the *Biographia Literaria* he says that the function of the fancy is to 'aggregate and associate, to evoke and combine' fixed and definite ideas; the imagination 'dissolves, diffuses, dissipates, in order to recreate'. It is important to note that in reacting against eighteenth-century rationalism Coleridge did not fall into the error of elevating the imagination above the reason. As

Shawcross says in his Introduction to the *Biographia Liter-aria*, Coleridge held by the 'truth, that the activity of the imagination is determined subjectively by the laws of our common sense, and objectively by the truth of things, and thus differs essentially from the accidental and seemingly capricious combinations of the fancy'. It is instructive, as he goes on to say, to compare Coleridge's aesthetic position with that of German Romanticism, as expressed by Friedrich von Schlegel: 'It is the beginning of all poetry to abolish the laws and methods of the rationally proceeding reason, and to plunge us once more into the ravishing confusions of fantasy, the original chaos of human nature.' Some English Romantics inclined to this German view; few understood with Words-worth and Coleridge that the poetic imagination was subject to valid laws of thought.

The difference the new theory of the imagination should have made to the interpretation of Milton's similes can be seen in Wordsworth's *Preface to Poems, 1815*, where he gives his own version of this famous distinction between the imagination and the fancy, and uses a simile from *Paradise Lost* as an example of true imaginative thinking – that same comparison of Satan to a fleet at sea on which I have previously quoted Zachary Pearce. Wordsworth says in effect that the fancy plays with superficial and accidental re-semblances between ideas and images to produce surprising or delightful combinations between disparate things; it does not attempt to modify or transform the materials with which it works but relies on simple juxtaposition; its effects are effects of comparison simply, of images laid side by side in the mind, and they last only while the images are thus kept together; there is no interfusion. In other words the fancy produces the sort of comparisons critics expect in a poetic simile. But when the imagination frames a comparison, though it may seem at first sight less striking and exact than a comparison of the fancy, 'a sense of the truth of the

[92]

likeness, from the moment it is perceived, grows – and continues to grow – upon the mind; the resemblance depending less upon outline and form of feature than upon expression and effect; less upon casual and outstanding, than upon inherent and internal, properties: moreover, the images invariably modify each other.' By the last observation, which is the gist of the argument, Wordsworth means that the image of the subject and the simile coalesce to produce something original. The imagination does not simply bring images together but works on them as plastic material; the imagination, in his own words, 'shapes and creates'.

I shall not discuss the validity of this theory of the creative imagination; enough for our purpose that it has been greeted as the gospel that freed us from the old neoclassical law. 'Creative' remains a blessed word for literary critics. Unfortunately the theory propounded by Coleridge and Wordsworth was immediately misconstrued in a Schlegelian sense: instead of a theory of imaginative reasoning a theory of the imagination freed from the reason prevailed. The romantic position merely reversed the neoclassical; the habit of regarding the reason and the imagination as opposing faculties continued, only the imagination was now exalted above the reason. Since criticism means reasoning about literature this left critics on the other horn of the neoclassical dilemma. And with regard to the similes of *Paradise Lost* all they could do was to go on repeating the Addisonian remarks, with the addition that Milton takes the opportunity of these digressions to display his learning and to introduce meaningless sonorous proper names, the latter being a game he is specially good at. Here are some samples from representative critics of the last three generations. Masson says we may remark in many of Milton's similes 'the habit, natural to the poetic mind, of pursuing a comparison, once suggested, beyond the mere limits of illustrative likeness, for the sake of a rich accumulation of circumstances beautiful in itself'. Raleigh says, 'His favourite figure is the "long-tailed" simile or, as it is better called, the decorative comparison, used for its ennobling rather than for its elucidating virtue.' Hanford says, 'A striking feature of Milton's style is his use of the epic or expanded simile. . . . These digressions are for him a welcome means of pouring forth the treasures of his mind.' Sherwin Proctor speaks of 'the detached or Homeric simile . . . presenting a single definite picture that is not directly part of the narrative or description'.[1]

The fact that this view has been so unanimous shows it to have some truth; and it is obvious enough that the variety of scene and incident introduced through these similes is one of their charms. And some poets have used them on occasion chiefly for the beauty of the independent pictures. A clear example is Arnold's *Sohrab and Rustum*, which may almost be said to exist poetically by virtue of its epic similes taken by themselves; and W. P. Ker rightly praises the poem on this account. The lines for instance describing the sign on Sohrab's shoulder can, perhaps, be fully enjoyed out of their context:

> as a cunning workman, in Pekin,
> Pricks with vermilion some clear porcelain vase,
> An emperor's gift – at early morn he paints,
> And all day long, and, when night comes, the lamp
> Lights up his studious forehead and thin hands –
> So delicately prick'd the sign appear'd
> On Sohrab's arm, the sign of Rustum's seal.

Long similes should always have this separable beauty but to regard this as their principal function is to take a super-

---

[1] James Whaler in *Compounding and Distribution of Similes in 'Paradise Lost'* M.P., 28, 1931, rejects the view that the similes are decorative, and says that they describe situations and illustrate the action; but his purpose and argument are narrower than mine.

ficial view. They are not so simply used in *Paradise Lost*. We have seen that this traditional view of the Miltonic simile arose from the like view of the Homeric simile, a view which, I am told, still prevails among classical scholars. R. C. Jebb, surprisingly enough, argued against it in his *Introduction to Homer* (1887), and I cannot do better than quote him in order to get round to a more reasonable and poetic point of view. 'The first point to observe', he wrote, 'is that the Homeric simile is not a mere ornament. It serves to introduce something which Homer desires to render exceptionally impressive. . . . Thus the Homeric similes are responses made on the narrator by the course of the narrative.' As to the method of the Homeric simile he quotes this example: 'When the sea-god Poseidon soars into the air from the Trojan plain, he is compared to a hawk,

> That from a beetling brow of rock
> Launched in mid air forth dashes to pursue
> Some lesser bird along the plain below.

Poseidon is not pursuing anyone; the point of the similitude is simply the speed through the air. But if A is to be made clearer by means of B, B itself must be clearly seen; and therefore Homer invests it with enough of detail to place a concrete image before the mind. The hawk to whom Poseidon is likened, is more vividly conceived when it is described as doing a particular act characteristic of a hawk, viz. pursuing another bird. . . . The object which furnishes the simile must be made distinct before the simile itself can be effective.' This gives the gist of what I have to say about Milton's similes. They answer the demands of the narrative; they are images used to portray the scenes and characters and events that compose the poem, picturings of the action, ideas and sentiments. They are what may be called transposed descriptions; and if they are to be effective, detail is as necessary as in direct descriptions. This is the first point;

[95]

but there is a second. Having been once used as similes the
images become, like any other poetic imagery, substantial
parts of the story, and the imaginative forces they release
have to be controlled and directed like any other factors
introduced into the story. They are not digressions the poet
can forget as soon as they are over; he cannot afford to
forget any image or word he uses, for each at once becomes
an element in the growing forces of his narrative. These are
the two chief points to be demonstrated.

I shall begin with two diverse examples of transposed
description from the first two Books of *Paradise Lost*, where
Milton uses a large number of these epic similes in portraying the fallen angels, their abode and their activities. They
are one of his main means of presenting scenes and figures
outside the range of human experience; and in order to
sustain both their strangeness and their sublimity he most
often chooses for analogy things also outside human experience, things fabulous or remote. It is obvious that such
analogies must be fully developed in order to work. Take
the first long simile in the poem, that describing Satan lying
outstretched on the burning lake:

> Thus *Satan* talking to his nearest Mate
> With Head up-lift above the wave, and Eyes
> That sparkling blaz'd, his other Parts besides
> Prone on the Flood, extended long and large
> Lay floating many a rood, in bulk as huge
> As whom the Fables name of monstrous size,
> *Titanian* or *Earth-born*, that warrd on *Jove*,
> *Briarios* or *Typhon*, whom the Den
> By ancient *Tarsus* held, or that Sea-beast
> *Leviathan*, which God of all his works
> Created hugest that Swim th' Ocean stream:
> Him haply slumbring on the *Norway* foam
> The Pilot of som small night-founderd Skiff,
> Deeming som Iland, oft, as Sea-men tell,
> With fixed Anchor in his scaly rinde

Moors by his side under the Lee, while Night
Invests the Sea, and wished Morn delays.
[i. 192–208

The ancient gods and giants lead up to the picture of the
Leviathan, and the following details are what is called
'pursuing a comparison beyond the limit of illustrative
likeness'. But what is it the poet has to do? Not just refer us
to a similar huge creature in the appropriate posture, so as
to instruct us that Satan was rather like that. He has to
depict, to make us see, to create a vision of immensity and
terror. The simile is not illustration but transposed description; for not only is Satan beyond human ken but so is the
fabulous Leviathan. 'Canst thou draw out leviathan with a
hook?' Suppose Milton had stopped short of the incident
of the skiff with its attendant circumstance, where then
would be the picture of Satan? To regard this picture as
something composed for its independent beauty is to draw
a false distinction between idea and image. The image of
the Leviathan, with all that creature's associations, is an
essential part of the creative process, and it remains a part
of our idea of Satan to the end of the story.

My second example is of the contrary case, where the
experience to be conveyed is not remote or fabulous but a
common human experience, and where the same appropriate strangeness and sublimity of effect are obtained by the
vast unlikeness in the things compared. It is the simile
describing the changed and cheerful state of mind in which
the fallen angels disperse from the infernal council after
Satan has taken on himself the promising but perilous
mission to earth:

Thus they thir doubtful consultations dark
Ended rejoicing in thir matchless Chief:
As when from mountain tops the dusky clouds
Ascending, while the North wind sleeps, orespread
Heav'ns cheerful face, the louring Element

Scowls ore the darkend lantskip Snow or showr;
If chance the radiant Sun with farewel sweet
Extend his ev'ning beam, the fields revive,
The birds thir notes renew, and bleating herds
Attest thir joy, that hill and valley rings.   [ii. 486–95

There is no logical connexion between the minds of devils
and an evening landscape, so that the usual quest for points
of comparison or their absence cannot even begin. The
simile moves straight to its proper task of description, a
vivid description of a mental experience transposed into
quite other but familiar terms. Does it not perfectly convey
happy deliverance from a gloomy conference such as most
of us have had experience of? One would have thought that
it was plain enough here that the description was entirely
contained in the simile, and that the picture must therefore
be completely worked out as in any other description; yet
here is Verity's note, representing the common view: 'This
simile is typical of many in Milton. . . . The peculiarity is
that he works the simile out, in all its bearings, into a picture
complete in itself but rather detached from the context.'
I am inclined to say, "Detached, my foot!"

This is an especially clear example of transposed description because the subject is a mental change and therefore the
train of ideas and emotions started by the simile are seen to
be strictly directed to portraying that change. But this
question of the train of ideas and emotions started by a simile
is far more complex than can be realized from an isolated
simile. In these two examples I have considered the simile
as a means of presenting single incidents, and as though
the effect stopped short with the occasion; but if the similes
really answer the needs of the narrative their effects will
extend beyond the immediate occasion, and we must consider their interactions and their continuing effects on the
course of the narrative. The similes become an organic part
of the imaginative structure, and we have to examine how

the poet organizes the imaginative movements they set going and fashions his narrative in accordance with them. I shall take for this purpose the series of similes that follow so thick and fast on each other at the close of Book I of the poem.

This Book has been devoted to presenting the fallen angels and their abode. Throughout Milton has been concerned to show his devils *as* devils but without derogating from their poetic dignity and appeal; to render them both heroic and monstrous, repulsive and contemptible yet at the same time impressive and alluring. One of his chief means is declared in the long roll-call of the devils, where he adopts the Christian tradition of identifying them with the pagan deities, oriental and classical. These legends lose nothing of their seductive beauty whilst being seen as loathsome:

> Thammuz came next behind,
> Whose annual wound in *Lebanon* allur'd
> The *Syrian* Damsels to lament his fate
> In amorous ditties all a Summers day,
> While smooth *Adonis* from his native Rock
> Ran purple to the Sea, suppos'd with blood
> Of *Thammuz* yearly wounded: the Love-tale
> Infected *Sions* daughters with like heat, ... [i.446–53

The last of these identifications comes after the building of Pandaemonium, at the point where the poet starts congregating his fiends at their new citadel, the topic that is to occupy the remainder of the Book. In these last seventy lines there are no less than five elaborate similes, taking up nearly half the total space. Here then is a good place to examine how Milton uses his similes in continuous narration, and how he composes them to make the story. I take the passage in three sections, beginning with the devils flocking to admire their new citadel:

D   [99]

The hasty multitude
Admiring enterd, and the work some praise
And some the Architect: his hand was known
In Heav'n by many a Towred structure high,
Where Scepterd Angels held thir residence,
And sat as Princes, whom the supreme King
Exalted to such power, and gave to rule,
Each in his Hierarchie, the Orders bright.
Nor was his name unheard or unador'd
In ancient *Greece*; and in *Ausonian* land
Men called him *Mulciber*; and how he fell
From Heav'n, they fabl'd, thrown by angry *Jove*
Sheer ore the Crystal Battlements: from Morn
To Noon he fell, from Noon to dewy Eve,
A Summers day; and with the setting Sun
Dropd from the Zenith like a falling Star,
On *Lemnos* th' *Aegaean* Ile: thus they relate,
Erring; for he with this rebellious rout
Fell long before. [i. 730–48

This description of Zeus pitching Hephaestus out of Heaven is a transposed description, being the first detailed, individual picture of the fall of the angels. And here we have the chance of observing how the poet handles his material. His source is the first *Iliad*. Hera is at cross purposes with Zeus, and her son Hephaestus warns her to be wary of trying a fall with the Father of Gods and Men: 'For the Olympian is an ill one to cross. I proved it once when, try as I might to save myself, he caught me by the foot and threw me from the threshold of Heaven; all day I fell headlong and with the · setting sun landed on Lemnos, and little breath was left in me by then. So spake Hephaestus.' And unquenchable laughter, Homer tells us, arose among the assembled Gods as they watched him bustle about on his lame leg, pouring wine for them. As Tillyard remarked, 'nothing could be further from Milton than this richly comic "source" '. Nevertheless Milton expects us to

[100]

remember the Homeric laughter at poor Hephaestus's expense. This anticipates the irony with which the whole story of the war in Heaven is told in Book VI; and it exemplifies the ridicule that underlies even his most enchanting pictures of the fallen angels. With whatever sad beauty he invests them he never permits us to forget their foolishness or 'the deep damnation of their taking off'. Those lines of lingering loveliness and regret,

> from Morn
> To Noon he fell, from Noon to dewy Eve,
> A Summers day

are followed by the blunt contemptuous statement

> thus they relate
> Erring.

Those who understand this alternation of the gentle and the stern understand Milton; here is the tenderness of the poetic mind, unseduced by the pathos it so exquisitely feels and portrays. Ruskin in his famous passage on the pathetic fallacy observes that the great poet feels strongly but also thinks strongly and sees truly: 'his mind is made up. . . . It is not this or that which will at once unbalance him. He is tender to impression at the surface, like a rock with deep moss on it; but there is too much mass of him to be moved. . . . Dante, in his most intense moods, has entire command of himself, and can look around calmly.' The words apply equally to Milton, who at the supreme moment of his story can make us feel the agony, the heartbreak of Adam's love for Eve, can make us sympathize wholeheartedly with his decision to sin with fallen Eve rather than desert her, and then can conclude

> he scrupl'd not to eat
> Against his better knowledge, not deceiv'd,
> But fondly overcome with Femal charm.   [ix. 997–9

This shocks your modern humanist, who has a touching faith in the sanctity of human weakness and folly. But this is to anticipate.

Part of the narrative value of this simile of Hephaestus, placed just where it is, is that it focuses in one memorable vision all the previous identifications of the fallen angels with the pagan deities before the poet moves on to the next incident. A general council is now summoned to Pandae-monium and the poet describes the congregating of the devils about their citadel:

> they anon
> With hunderds and with thousands trooping came
> Attended: all access was throngd, the Gates
> And Porches wide, but chief the spacious Hall
> (Though like a coverd field, where Champions bold
> Wont ride in armd, and at the Soldans chair
> Defi'd the best of *Panim* chivalry
> To mortal combat or career with Lance)
> Thick swarmd, both on the ground and in the air,
> Brusht with the hiss of russling wings. As Bees
> In spring time, when the Sun with *Taurus* rides,
> Pour forth thir populous youth about the Hive
> In clusters; they among fresh dews and flowers
> Flie to and fro, or on the smoothed Plank,
> The Suburb of thir Straw-built Cittadel,
> New rubd with Baum, expatiate and conferr
> Thir State affairs. So thick the aerie crowd
> Swarmd and were straitend.   [i. 759–76

First comes the parenthetical and seemingly irrelevant comparison of the hall to the lists of chivalric encounters; its point is that it refers us back to an earlier identification of Satan's marshalled hosts with the joustings and battles of medieval romance:

> and what resounds
> In Fable or Romance of *Uthers* Son
> Begirt with *Brittish* and *Armoric* Knights;

And all who since, Baptiz'd or Infidel
Jousted in *Aspramont* or *Montalban*,
Damasco, or *Marocco*, or *Trebisond*,
Or whom *Biserta* sent from *Afric* shore
When *Charlemain* with all his Peerage fell
By *Fontarabbia*.   [i. 579–87

As Ruskin said, 'What a delicious sound of splintering
lances there is in the single line, "Jousted in Aspramont or
Montalban!"' And what a thud and ripple of hooves in
the next line! And then, with this spacious image in our
minds, the swarm of devils is suddenly reduced to a vision
of bees about their hive. The transition is effected through
the sibilants:

Brusht with the hiss of russling wings.. As Bees
In spring time . . .

The commentators refer to the same simile in the *Iliad* and
the *Aeneid*, but the interesting point is not that Milton
borrows the image but how he puts it to his own account.
He has to describe the thronging of his gigantic devils, something beyond the scope of the human imagination; we just
cannot picture a swarming host of giants except through
the wrong end of the telescope; the transformation to bees
adjusts his colossal fiends to the focus of human attention.
Once again the primary purpose of the simile is a transposed
description answering the exact needs of the story. And once
again each detail has its ironic undertone as well as its
descriptive aptness and charm, culminating in the satiric
stroke,

                                        expatiate and conferr
Thir State affairs.

The delicacy with which Milton ridicules without disgracing
his devils, without sacrificing their poetic appeal, is a point
those might note who deny him wit.

[103]

The way has now been prepared for the actual transformation scene: having reduced the devils in our eyes to
bees he can now present them as human dwarfs and pygmies:

> till the Signal giv'n,
> Behold a wonder ! they but now who seemd
> In bigness to surpass. Earths Giant Sons
> Now less than smallest Dwarfs, in narrow room
> Throng numberless, like that Pigmean Race
> Beyond the *Indian* Mount, or Faerie Elves
> Whose midnight Revels by a Forrest side
> Or Fountain some belated Peasant sees,
> Or dreams he sees, while over-head the Moon
> Sits Arbitress, and nearer to the Earth
> Wheels her pale course, they on thir mirth and dance
> Intent, with jocond Music charm his ear;
> At once with joy and fear his heart rebounds.
> Thus incorporeal Spirits to smallest forms
> Reduc'd thir shapes immense, and were at large,
> Though without number still amidst the Hall
> Of that infernal Court.   [i. 776–92

Which is direct description and which simile here?

C. S. Lewis in his *Preface to 'Paradise Lost'* offers his own
variation on the customary view of Milton's similes, with
some comments on the second of the above similes, in a
passage where he is drawing a distinction between what he
calls the ostensible or logical and the emotional or covert
connexions between Milton's images: 'The Miltonic simile
does not always illustrate what it pretends to be illustrating.
The likeness between the two things being compared is often
trivial, and is, indeed, required only to save the face of the
logical censor. At the end of Book I the fiends are compared to elves. Smallness is the only point of resemblance.
The first use of the simile is to provide contrast and relief,
to refresh us by transition from Hell to a moonlit English
lane.' It is surprising that the author of *The Allegory of Love*

has momentarily forgotten that the land of fairy is the medieval version of the classical Hades; as in the lay of *Sir Orfeo* for instance, where the Knight wins back his Dame Erodys from the 'lond of faërië' by his minstrelsy, as Orpheus half won back Eurydice from Hades. For Milton too fairies and elves belong with those mortals of pagan superstition whom, along with the nymphs and fauns and satyrs of classical mythology, he identifies with his lesser devils. Smallness is certainly not the only point of resemblance between fiends and fairies. Fairies *were* fiends, however charming and bewitching in the older as well as the modern senses of both words. This ambiguous appeal of fairies is expressed in the concluding line of the simile:

At once with joy and fear his heart rebounds.

The latter part of Milton's *Ode on the Nativity* is an early sketch for the elaborate account of the fallen angels in *Paradise Lost*; there he celebrates Christ's triumph over the heathen gods of ancient civilization, Greece and Rome, Egypt and Asia Minor, and lastly

the yellow-skirted Fays
Fly after the Night-steeds, leaving their Moon-lov'd
maze.

Similarly Comus, initiating the rites he and his crew are about to celebrate, invokes 'the pert fairies and the dapper elves' along with the other assistants to their obscene revels. And so here, in the simile in *Paradise Lost*, the poet is describing magic and forbidden rites which, like those of Lapland witches, draw down the watching moon. What better simile could there be for presenting Milton's hilarious Lilliputian devils? This is the primary purpose of the simile — to present the scene, not just to 'provide contrast and relief, to refresh us by a transition from Hell to a moonlit English lane'. Lewis's 'moonlit English lane' substitutes,

[105]

in James Joyce's phrase, a 'Lawn Tennyson' scene for Milton's thrilling encounter within the purlieus of Hell. And why, one asks, should we need relief and refreshment from Milton's Hell? Do we not enjoy it?

There remains one last proof, in the concluding lines of the Book, of the functional value of this simile:

> But far within
> And in thir own dimensions like themselves
> The great Seraphic Lords and Cherubim
> In close recess and secret conclave sat
> A thousand Demi-Gods on golden seats,
> Frequent and full.   [i. 792–7

On these lines I cannot do better than quote Lewis again: 'It is by contrast with the fairies that these councillors have grown so huge, and by contrast with the fanciful image that the hush before their debate becomes so intense, and it is by that intensity that we are so well prepared for the opening of Book II.' I object only to 'fanciful' in this pointed criticism.

Chapter 5

SIMILES FROM VOYAGES OF DISCOVERY

It will have become apparent that one of the principles of imaginative logic in Milton's similes is the appropriation of certain topics or fields of comparison to particular characters and themes, so that they become symbols for those characters and themes. This is one of the means by which he makes plain the course and meaning of his story, and by which he holds the immense structure of his poem firmly together. It can be best illustrated by a group of similes used for Satan's main exploit.

In the first place it is significant that many of these similes are drawn from the Orient, from the Near and the Far East. The reason is that Milton, like his contemporaries, thought of the East as the home of despotism, the scene of worldly pride and ambition, of barbaric luxury, cruelty and lust, of idolatry and dark superstitions; as representing all that in politics, morals, and religion was most abhorrent to his mind. It is summed up in the one word 'Asiatic', which had meant uncivilized to the Greeks also. And Asia was the name not only for the Near and Far East but for Egypt and the whole of Africa; and also for America, since Columbus had at first supposed that he had discovered not the West but the East Indies. The East meant in fact everywhere outside Christendom. Another name for this outer world was Ind or India. Purchas says that 'India doth now signify all the Easterne World in vulgar appelation . . . India is a name given to any remote, rich, and strange Region very much differing from ours, as the Mexico, Brazil, Malaca, &c.'[1]

And so Satan takes on the guise of an oriental tyrant. The note is struck firmly at the opening of Book II, when the 'great consult' begins:

> High on a Throne of Royal State, which far
> Outshon the wealth of *Ormus* and of *Ind*,
> Or where the gorgeous East with richest hand
> Showrs on her Kings *Barbaric* Pearl and Gold,
> *Satan* exalted sat. [ii. 1–5

Ormus is an example of what has happened to so many of Milton's contemporary allusions. To the uninstructed reader today it is only an example of Milton's trick of using exotic names, used merely for the sound and signifying nothing; but in Milton's day it meant as much as London or New York or other wealthy cities and trading centres do to the modern reader. Ormuz, at the mouth of the Persian Gulf, lying at the crossroads between East and West, was the great mart of the world. Ralph Fitch, the earliest English traveller and trader in Mesopotamia, said in 1583: 'In this towne are merchants of all Nations. . . . Here is very great trade of all sorts of spices, drugs, silke, fine tapestries of Persia, great store of pearles which come from the Isle of Baharim, and are the best pearles of all others, and many horses of Persia, which serve all India' (Hakluyt, iii. 284). Purchas writes: 'And so the Inhabiters of Hormuz doe say,

---

[1] In the following account of the voyages of exploration and discovery in the sixteenth and seventeenth centuries I have used chiefly Hakluyt's *Principal Navigations* and *Purchas His Pilgrimes*. I have also drawn on William Foster's *England's Quest of the Eastern Trade* and *English Factories in India*, and J. Courtenay Locke's *The First Englishmen in India*; but I am primarily indebted to a brilliant review of these books by Edward Thomas in *The Times Literary Supplement*, 30 March 1933, which has, I believe, never been reprinted.

that all the world is a ring, and Hormuz is the stone of it,
Whereby it is commonly said that the Custome-house of
Hormuz is a channel of Silver which alwaies runneth.'

Nowadays trading may not strike us as romantic or heroic,
but in the sixteenth and seventeenth centuries the great
voyages of discovery recorded by Hakluyt and Purchas
were undertaken by merchant adventurers in pursuit of
trade. Milton uses these voyages magnificently to describe
Satan's hazardous voyage to Earth. This throws light incidentally on the old problem of who is the hero of the poem.
The paradox that Satan is the hero stultifies, as I have
previously said, Milton's whole intention in the poem; yet
in a sense it remains true, as W. P. Ker said, that 'Satan has
all the heroism to himself, that is all the contending power'.
This is true if we take 'heroic' in the traditional sense; but
Milton, as we have seen, had a different conception of the
heroic. Yet the fact remains that Satan is the only character
capable of expressing the heroism of human endeavour not
only in war but in what for Milton was a more glorious
field of action – the struggle with nature, the search for
knowledge, the exploration of the world. The age to which
Milton belonged was just such an age of heroic endeavour
and achievement – the revival of learning and the advance-
ment of science, the geographical discoveries, the assertion
of religious and political freedom, all reveal the aspiring
spirit of the age; and Milton, who was a man of his time,
could not leave this out of his poem. Yet some of it could
only be expressed through Satan and his exploits. In particular the voyages of discovery and the struggle for sea power
in pursuit of trade provided contemporary material galore,
of the traditional kind, for an heroic poem. The Portuguese
poet Camoens had already made Vasco da Gama's doubling
of the Cape of Good Hope and discovery of the sea-route to
India the main episode of his national epic. And so, as
Satan starts on his flight towards the gates of Hell and his

hazardous quest for the new world of man, Milton calls up
this vision of a voyage from India to the Cape:

> As when farr off at Sea a Fleet descri'd
> Hangs in the Clouds, by *Æquinoctial* winds
> Close sailing from *Bengala*, or the Iles
> Of *Ternate* and *Tidore*, whence Merchants bring
> Thir spicie Drugs: they on the Trading Flood
> Through the wide *Ethiopian* to the Cape
> Ply stemming nightly toward the Pole. So seemd
> Far off the flying Fiend.   [ii. 636–43

'What simile', exclaimed Tennyson, 'was ever so vast as
this?'

Bentley, in his less poetic manner, touches as usual on
most of the points in the passage that call for elucidation:
'This long and tedious comparison is so silly here and ped-
antical, quite improper for the Place. . . . And why those
exotic Names, *Bengála, Térnate* and *Tidóre*? a vain Ostenta-
tion of the most vulgar Knowledge; when a ship at home in
our own Channel would serve the turn better. *Trade Winds*
indeed I have heard of, but *Trading Flood* I learn first here.
But why must the *Aethiopic* Sea be it? when the *Europaean*
Seas carry ten times the Trade. And why is all this done
Nightly, to contradict the whole Account? since at that time
a Sail cannot be *descried*.' All these questions need answering: indeed, if the lines seemed pedantic, exotic, and
ostentatious to Bentley, small wonder they should seem so
to the modern reader, for Bentley was so much nearer to
the world they portray. In fact the words he questions are
vibrant with meaning, which must be recovered for the
poetry to come fully to life.

The proper names were anything but exotic or unfamiliar
at the time; nor are they just good musical noises, the usual
explanation of Milton's proper names. Their first function
is to plot the course of the voyage from the estuary of the

Ganges to the Spice Islands and then across the Indian Ocean ('the wide *Ethiopian*', so called in antiquity and by Purchas) to the Cape of Good Hope; and they show Milton's grasp of the contemporary history he was alluding to. Some of the earliest English trading stations were along the Bengal estuary and down the Coromandel coast of India. Ternate and Tidore were two of the Spice Islands in the Malay Archipelago; and these names would bring to mind the whole saga of sea exploration, and to Englishmen the most famous voyage of all, Drake's circumnavigation of the globe in 1577–80. The account of how Drake on his homeward journey intended to touch at Tidore but was persuaded by the rival King of Ternate to put in there instead makes the main episode in this part of the story as printed in Hakluyt. Drake concluded a treaty with the King of Ternate which the East India Company later appealed to in claiming prior rights over the Dutch in the East Indies. In 1605 the Company established trading stations in many of the Spice Islands, and from then on they figure frequently in the Company's correspondence and in the warfare waged first with the Portuguese and the Dutch for naval and commercial supremacy in these waters, and later with the Dutch alone, when the Portuguese had lost their initial advantage in the East Indies. In 1623 the English factory at Amboyna, one of the Spice Islands, was destroyed by the Dutch, the English shipping being sunk and fearful tortures inflicted on the English traders; in 1652 Milton, as Cromwell's Foreign Secretary, drew up the claims for compensation on account of the Massacre of Amboyna and of later depredations on English merchant shipping. Even in the next generation this incident was still remembered by the public, for in 1673, at a time when we were at war with the Dutch, Dryden produced his occasional tragedy, *Amboyna, or The Cruelties of the Dutch to the English Merchants.*

'Spicie Drugs' were a more valuable cargo and included

more commodities than one would suppose. They included of course the spices so important at the time for both seasoning food and pickling meat for winter consumption; the chief of these were cloves, mace, nutmeg, pepper, ginger and sugar. But they comprehended also all ingredients used not only in pharmacy and dyeing but also in the mechanical arts, if brought from a far country; it also covered cocoa and coffee when they appeared. (See Lyttleton's *Latin-English Dictionary*, 1677–1723, stated to be based partly on 'a large MS. in Three Volumes of John Milton'; and *Chamber's Cyclopaedia*, 1727–51). 'Spicie Drugs' in fact means the whole of the wealthiest commerce of the times.

Trading, as I have said, no longer appears to us either dangerous or heroic, and we need to remind ourselves that it was not always a peaceful pursuit. The history of the sixteenth and seventeenth centuries was very much that of the struggle between the nations of Europe, especially Spain, Portugal, Holland, France, and England, for possession not only of the Americas and their wealth but even more for possession of the East. Milton was well acquainted with these affairs not only from his reading in Hakluyt and Purchas, and as matters of common talk, but from being engaged in them as Latin Secretary during the Commonwealth. All English vessels at sea, in home as well as foreign waters, were treated as enemies by their Dutch rivals and as pirates by the Spanish and Portuguese, who claimed to hold the East as well as the West in fee from the Pope.

As Secretary to Cromwell, Milton writes in August 1656 to Louis XIV, complaining of a French attack on the English ship *Endeavour*: 'Laden at *Teneriff* with three hunder'd Pipes of rich Canary . . . was taken by Four *French* Vessels, seeming Ships of Burthen, but fitted and mann'd like Privateers, under the Command of *Giles de la Roche* their Admiral, and carri'd with all her Freight, and the greatest part of the Seamen to the *East Indies*, whither he pretended

[112]

to be bound (Fourteen excepted, who were put ashore on the Coast of *Guinney*) which the said *Giles* said he did with Intent, that none of 'em might escape from so Remote and Barbarous a Countrey to do him harm by their Testimony ... well knowing there was a firm Peace at that time between the *French* and our Republic.'

The seas moreover were swarming with pirates, and nowhere more than in the delta of the Ganges. Well might the poet imagine his merchantmen as 'Close sailing from *Bengala*', this being usually interpreted as sailing in close convoy for safety and mutual aid. Another interpretation, which does not contradict but reinforces the same general sense, is 'sailing close-hauled into the wind'. Milton's '*Æquinoctial* Winds' are of course the trade winds or monsoons, which blow steadily north-east or south-west at fixed periods of the year. Those sailing from Bengal to the Cape would wish to sail before the wind; but if they waited for the favourable trade wind from the north-east they would meet the contrary south-west wind after crossing the Equator. So that they must sail into the wind for either the first or second part of the voyage. The meaning 'close-hauled' gains support from the word 'Ply', which may well mean here 'To beat against the wind; to tack, work to windward'. The word is used constantly in this sense by Hakluyt and Purchas: 'But being late in the monson, streames and winds both against us, with much toyle to ship and men wee plied several leagues from Bantam, and could get no further from the tenth of this moneth (January) to the first of March. ... For it is great odds, when a man may sayle thirtie six leagues in foure and twentie houres, and will sayle but foure close upon a wind' (Purchas, iv. pp. 80 and 90).

Here the phrase 'streames and winds both against us' suggests another meaning for Milton's 'Trading Flood'. The accepted interpretation is that 'Flood' means 'sea' and 'Trading' means 'trade winds'; so that the words mean 'the

[113]

seas where the trade winds blow', a weak repetition of '*Æquinoctial* Winds'. 'Flood' however could mean 'stream' in the sense in which it is used by Purchas above, or as in 'Gulf Stream', namely the sea-current on which ships had to rely as much as on the trade-winds. 'Stemming' probably means here 'making headway with difficulty against tide, current or wind'; in which sense it is used of flying as well as sailing. The meaning 'sailing against both wind and current' contributes to the force of the simile by suggesting the difficulty and labour of Satan's flight.

'Nightly' has a significance which Bentley's prosaic mind misses. Early navigators relied on the pole star for navigating by night; but when a ship had crossed the Line, as Milton's fleet does, there was no prominent star near the South Pole to serve as a guide, and in these circumstances 'stemming nightly' was another of the hazards with which mariners had to contend.

Even more formidable than the known and certain dangers of these voyages was the dread with which seamen's imaginations were affected as they sailed towards what might be the southern edge of the world, and which Coleridge was to recreate in *The Ancient Mariner* from narratives like those from which I have been quoting. Sir George Birdwood, in the *Register of East India Company Letters*, writes: 'The Portuguese, and the Dutch and English who first adventured after them into the Southern hemisphere and round the utmost horn of Africa, were still haunted all through the fifteenth, sixteenth and even seventeenth centuries by the old superstition that they were descending into Hades. . . . A tract of stormy sea might be the start of a flood that would suck them into the abyss. Night, carrying unfamiliar stars, was a terrifying spectacle.' This vast terror is conveyed in Milton's two lines:

> Through the wide *Ethiopian* to the Cape
> Ply stemming nightly toward the Pole.

The vision of Satan starting on the flight that will take him through the unexplored abyss of Chaos has called up in Milton's imagination a parallel voyage no less awe-inspiring. His voyage fittingly concludes with the lines:

> And like a weather-beaten Vessel holds
> Gladly the Port, though Shrouds and Tackle torn;
> Or in the emptier waste, resembling Air,
> Weighs his spred wings, . . .   [ii. 1043–6

The last words, incidentally, provide the first example in the poem of Milton's keen observation of birds. Anyone who has watched the majestic sailing of an eagle over a battle-field, with wings outspread but not perceptibly moving, will recognize the exact meaning of 'weighs'. This and other descriptions of birds in the poem, to which I shall call attention, refutes the idea that Milton's weak eyesight prevented close observation of the natural world.

I began with Bentley's observations on this simile. That we have not got beyond Bentley, though we wrap it up more, can be seen from Verity's comment, a representative one: 'Note here how the simile is worked out, beyond the precise point of comparison; how also the proper names convey an impression of mysterious remoteness.'

These seafaring similes are pretty numerous in *Paradise Lost*, all of them, I think, in connexion with Satan or his associates. Not the least striking of them is that used to describe the building by Sin and Death of the causeway connecting Hell with Earth, just before Satan returns to them in triumph. Among the voyages of discovery none had been more hazardous and heroic than the many attempts by Englishmen to find an alternative north-east or north-west passage through Arctic seas to the rich and fabulous Cathay or China, and so to the East Indies. The hardships and perils faced by these intrepid men can be read of in the matter-of-fact narratives in Hakluyt and Purchas. One sentence will set the picture: 'We met with much driving Yce ... the whole place being frozen over from the one side to the other, and as it were with walles, mountaines, and bulwarks of yce, choked up the passage, and denied us entrance.' The first expedition to the north-east set out in three ships under Sir Hugh Willoughby in 1553: one was wrecked; one received 'such a blow with a rock of yce that she sunk downe therewith in the sight of the whole fleete', and the whole crew perished from hunger and cold. The English agent at Moscow eventually sent to recover the ship with its dead, but 'it sunk by the way with all thir Dead, and them also that brought it'. On his second venture Sir Hugh himself was shipwrecked and drowned off the Scottish coast on his way home. Hakluyt wrote: 'He commits his life (a thing to a man of all things most deare) to the raging Sea, and the uncertainty of many dangers. We shall here rest at home quietly with our friends and acquaintance.' One expedition after another went out in the sixteenth and seventeenth centuries, but none on the north-east passage succeeded in penetrating beyond the mouth of the Petsora river in northern Russia.

In his *Brief History of Moscovia*, published in 1682 but, as he himself tells us, 'writ by the Author's own hand before he lost his sight', Milton summarizes the story of Sir Hugh's first journey to Moscow, as printed in Hakluyt; all his references in the *History* are to Hakluyt and Purchas. But not only did he read of such things but must have witnessed similar scenes to that described in Hakluyt of the departure of Sir Hugh's fleet: 'And being come neere to Greenewich, (where the Court lay) presently upon the newes thereof, the Courtiers came running out, and the common people flockt together, standing very thicke upon the shoare: the Privie Councel, they lookt out at the windowes of the Court, and the rest ranne up to the toppes of the towers: the shippes hereupon discharge their Ordinance,

[116]

and shoote off their pieces after the maner of warre, and of the sea, insomuch that the tops of the hilles sounded therewith, the valleys and waters gave an Eccho, and the mariners, they shouted in such sort, that the Skie rang again with the noyse thereof. . . . To be short, it was a very triumph.' Milton says of this voyage: 'The discovery of *Russia* by the northern Ocean, made first, of any Nation we know, by *English* men, might have seem'd an enterprise almost heroick; if any higher end then the excessive love of Gaine and Traffic, had animated the design. Nevertheless that in regard that many things not unprofitable to the knowledge of Nature, and other Observations are hereby come to light, as good events ofttimes arise from evil occasions, it will not be the worst labour to relate briefly the beginning, and prosecution of this adventurous Voiage; untill it became at last a familiar Passage.' This shows Milton's ambivalent view of these heroic exploits, and explains how he was able to use them in presenting those of the Evil One. Not least among their contributions to 'knowledge of Nature', for which he valued them, was that of geography: 'The study of Geography', he says in *Of Education,* 'is both profitable and delightful.'

The causeway built by Sin and Death 'over the waste Wide Anarchie of Chaos' could not be more directly and powerfully described than in the simile of the explorers of the difficult and desolate Arctic seas:

Solid or slimie, as in raging Sea
Tost up and down, together crowded drove
From each side shoaling towards the mouth of Hell.
As when two Polar Winds blowing adverse
Upon the *Cronian* Sea, together drive
Mountains of Ice, that stop th' imagind way
Beyond *Petsora* Eastward, to the rich
Cathaian Coast.   [x. 285–93

[117]

Chapter 6

GOD AND SATAN

Coming now to the main business of examining the action
of the poem I shall pass over the first two Books as the ones
most have read; some, having read so far in those abomin-
able school editions containing Books I and II only, read no
further, which is sufficient reason for their thinking Satan
the hero. I shall deal first with God and Satan as presented
in Book III and the opening of Book IV; then with the revolt
of the angels and with the war in Heaven in Books V and
VI, and with Satan's return to Hell in Book X; then with
the Creation as related in Book VII; and finally with the
central story of Adam and Eve.

Book III takes us from Satan on the outside of the new
world of man, after his perilous voyage through Chaos, to
God in Heaven. Here is the only place in the poem where the
three themes of the story – Heaven, Hell and Earth – are
brought into immediate conjunction, are seen in one *coup
d'œil*. The issue is fairly joined. We look down with God
on Adam and Eve – our first far-off sight of them, for previously we have only heard rumours of them – and on Satan
making his way towards them:

> On Earth he first beheld
> Our two first Parents, yet the onely two
> Of mankind, in the happie Garden plac't,
> Reaping immortal fruits of joy and love,
> Uninterrupted joy, unrivald love
> In blissful solitude; he then surveyd
> Hell and the Gulf between, and *Satan* there

Coasting the wall of Heav'n on this side Night
In the dun Air sublime, and ready now
To stoop with wearied wings and willing feet
On the bare outside of this World, . . .   [iii. 64–74

The placing of the reader at this central point of view at this
juncture in the story is an example of Milton's mastery of
narrative method.

It is usually thought that the scenes in Heaven are colour-
less and insipid after the scenes in Hell, and that the poet's
heart is not in it. Nothing could be further from the truth.
The realization of Heaven is one of Milton's most astonishing poetical feats. If we remember that the free invention
and the varied imagery used in describing Hell are debarred
him in describing Heaven we shall begin to appreciate his
achievement. Is there anything finer in Dante than these
lines describing God in Heaven?

About him all the Sanctities of Heaven
Stood thick as Starrs, and from his sight receiv'd
Beatitude past utterance.   [iii. 60–62

Milton's God, as I have said, appears a merely legalistic
God because he is represented for the most part as pro-
nouncing decrees, judgments, and punishments, whilst
his mercy, grace and love are expressed through his Son:

Beyond compare the Son of God was seen
Most glorious, in him all his Father shon
Substantially exprest, and in his face
Divine compassion visibly appear'd,
Love without end, and without measure Grace, . . .
                                          [iii. 138–42

This too is Milton's God; and although for narrative purposes Father and Son are necessarily presented as two
characters, we are not thereby justified in censuring his idea
of God whilst approving the Son,

In whom the fulness dwells of love divine,   [iii. 225

and through whom the Father is manifested and acts. No
one with an ear for verse can read the words in which the
Son accepts the sacrifice laid on him by the Father for man's
redemption, and believe that Milton is insensible to the
ardour of divine love; nor on the other hand can anyone
who reads the words in which the Father accepts the bitter
sacrifice:

> O thou in Heav'n and Earth the only peace
> Found out for mankind under wrauth, O thou
> My sole complacence ! well thou knowst how dear
> To me are all my works, nor Man the least
> Though last created, that for him I spare
> Thee from my bosom and right hand, to save,
> By losing thee a while, the whole Race lost.
> Thou therefore whom thou only canst redeem,
> Thir Nature also to thy Nature join;
> . . . So Man, as is most just,
> Shall satisfie for Man, be judg'd and die,
> And dying rise, and rising with him raise
> His Brethren, ransomd with his own dear life.
> So Heav'nly love shall outdoo Hellish hate, . . .
>
> [iii. 274–98

Here the verse lifts in response to the passionate feeling; it
is in a very different strain from the purely doctrinal
speeches, even though it is itself doctrinal.

Nor is it true that Milton fails to express the joy of
Heaven. The hymn of the angelic host to the Father and
Son is jubilant poetry such as only Milton among English
poets can write on spiritual themes; here again he rivals
Dante. The joy of the angels, unlike the joy of the devils at
the close of the council in Hell, cannot be expressed in
simile; it has to be expressed directly or through the simple
imagery of light, and above all through the music and
orchestration of the verse:

Thee Father first they sung Omnipotent,
Immutable, Immortal, Infinite,
Eternal King; thee Author of all being,
Fountain of Light, thyself invisible
Amidst the glorious brightness where thou sitst
Thron'd inaccessible, but when thou shad'st
The full blaze of thy beams, and through a cloud
Drawn round about thee like a radiant Shrine,
Dark with excessive bright thy skirts appear,
Yet dazle Heav'n, that brightest Seraphim
Approach not, but with both wings veil thir eyes.
Thee next they sang of all Creation first,
Begotten Son, Divine Similitude,
In whose conspicuous count'nance, without cloud
Made visible, th' Almighty Father shines,
Whom else no Creature can behold; on thee
Imprest th' effulgence of his Glorie abides,
Transfus'd on thee his ample Spirit rests.
Hee Heav'n of Heavens and all the Powers therein
By thee created, and by thee threw down
Th' aspiring Dominations: . . . .
No sooner did thy dear and onely Son
Perceive thee purposd not to doom frail Man
So strictly, but much more to pittie enclin'd,
Hee to appease thy wrauth, and end the strife
Of Mercy and Justice in thy face discernd,
Regardless of the Bliss wherein he sat
Second to thee, offerd himself to die
For mans offence. O unexampl'd love,
Love nowhere to be found less than Divine!
Hail Son of God, Saviour of Men, thy Name
Shall be the copious matter of my Song
Henceforth, and never shall my Harp thy praise
Forget, nor from thy Fathers praise disjoin.   [iii. 372–415

T. S. Eliot says that Milton is a musical poet; this is certainly
true, though the implication that he had no other poetical
gift in a high degree is not.

The second movement of the poem ends here in the middle of Book III. Apart from the episode of the war in Heaven it is the longest of the scenes in Heaven. We return now to Satan on the outside of our universe:

> Thus they in Heav'n, above the starry Sphear,
> Thir happie hours in joy and hymning spent.
> Mean while upon the firm opacous Globe
> Of this round World, whose first convex divides
> The luminous inferior Orbs, enclos'd
> From *Chaos* and th' inroad of Darkness old,
> *Satan* alighted walks: a Globe farr off
> It seemd, now seems a boundless Continent
> Dark, waste, and wild, under the frown of Night
> Starless expos'd, . . .   [iii. 416–25

'Starless expos'd' shows Milton's peculiar strength of imagination in realizing the cosmic spaces: one wonders how it can be said that he has no visual imagination. The further value of the phrase will be found when Satan looks down through the star-littered universe, and again when he looks up from earth at the sun-filled sky. There follows a simile symbolizing Satan and his purpose. At the end of Book II, after the victorious conclusion to his heroic voyage of exploration, he is likened to an eagle as he surveyed the scene beneath: he is now likened to a vulture. Birds of prey are obvious images for Satan but they are always vivid images; whether the bird is eagle or vulture or cormorant, it is always nicely observed and portrayed.

> As when a Vultur on *Imaus* bred,
> Whose snowie ridge the roving *Tartar* bounds,
> Dislodging from a Region scarce of prey
> To gorge the flesh of Lambs or yeanling Kids
> On Hills where Flocks are fed, flies toward the Springs
> Of *Ganges* or *Hydaspes*, *Indian* streams;
> But in his way lights on the barren Plains
> Of *Sericana*, where *Chineses* drive

With Sails and Wind thir canie Waggons light:
So on this windie Sea of Land, the Fiend
Walkd up and down alone bent on his prey, . . .
[iii. 431–41

Such panoramic descriptions are needed by Milton's subject,
and they are within the scope of the writer's art, though not
to the same extent of the painter's; this is a landscape proper
only to literature. Hazlitt says, 'If Milton had taken a
journey for the express purpose, he could not have described this scenery and mode of life better. Such passages
are like demonstrations of natural history.' But what I particularly wish to draw attention to is that it is another example
of Milton's close observation of the stance and movements
of birds, not the easiest of subjects for a supposedly purblind
man's observation. The single word 'dislodging' makes one
see and feel the heavy obscene droop of the vulture and its
falling rather than springing into flight; an impression
reinforced by 'gorge' at the same position in the next line.

The digression that now occurs on the Paradise of Fools
is a brilliant polemic against the Roman Church, reminding
us of the similar outburst in *Lycidas*. Those who object to
its ferocity should reflect that this sort of thing is less frequent
in Milton's poetry than in Dante's *Divina Commedia*. Nor
do I know why one should not enjoy the devastating power
of this satire, as one enjoys Pope or Swift, without bothering
about its uncharitableness; satire *is* uncharitable, and hatred
is proper to poetry as one of the universal passions. What
seems a more serious objection to the passage, at first sight,
is that it is out of keeping with the dignity of epic, offends
against decorum; but there is nothing out of keeping, for
this is satire in the grand style. Nor does it interrupt the
narrative, or disillusion us of our imaginary habitation of the
outside of the human universe, since the poet can introduce
his summary description of that universe into the middle of
his diatribe:

[123]

> They pass the Planets sev'n, and pass the fixt,
> And that Crystallin Sphear whose ballance weighs
> The Trepidation talkt, and that first mov'd.
>
> [iii. 481–3

These lines prepare for the next move in the story – Satan's flight through the universe.

Milton now uses his device of reminiscence as he invariably does on resuming the main story after some major interlude such as that of the scene in Heaven. As Satan stands at the opening of the human world and

> Looks down with wonder at the sudden view
> Of all this World at once
>
> [iii. 542–3

we remember him standing on the verge of Chaos at the start of his adventure. The wonder of Creation holds him at his first sight of it; the word 'wonder' is repeated after the simile of the scout:

> As when a Scout
> Through dark and desert ways with peril gone
> All night; at last by break of cheerful dawn
> Obtains the brow of some high-climbing Hill,
> Which to his eye discovers unaware
> The goodly prospect of som forren land
> First-seen, or some renownd Metropolis
> With glistering Spires and Pinnacles adornd,
> Which now the Rising Sun gilds with his beams.
> Such wonder seiz'd, though after Heaven seen,
> The Spirit malign, but much more envy seiz'd
> At sight of all this World beheld so fair.
> Round he surveys, and well might, where he stood
> So high above the circling Canopie
> Of Nights extended shade; from Eastern Point
> Of *Libra* to the fleecie Starr that bears
> Andromeda farr off *Atlantic* seas
> Beyond th' *Horizon*.
>
> [iii. 543–60

Verity takes occasion to comment on this passage: 'No poet,

I think, conveys a sense of vast distance so acutely as does Milton, perhaps from his blindness.' But why drag in his blindness? This is not a case of blindness but of vision.

There follows the description of Satan's smooth downward flight through the universe, recalling by contrast the earlier battling of his way up through Chaos. The contrast is not only in the words but in the movement of the verse:

> then from Pole to Pole
> He views in bredth, and without longer pause
> Down right into the Worlds first Region throws
> His flight precipitant, and windes with ease
> Through the pure marble Air his oblique way
> Amongst innumerable Starrs, that shon
> Stars distant, but nigh hand seemd other Worlds,
> Or other Worlds they seemd or happy Iles, . . .
>
> [iii. 560–7

The movement of the verse perfectly follows the swerving, gull-like swoop of Satan. Milton describes not only flight but all bodily movement with the true thrill of sensation: this too is 'sensation', which T. S. Eliot would deny his writing.

After receiving directions from Uriel, Regent of the Sun, Satan

> Took leave, and toward the coast of Earth beneath,
> Down from th' Ecliptic, sped with hop't success,
> Throws his steep flight in many an Aerie wheel,
> Nor stayd, till on *Niphates* top he lights.
>
> [iii. 739–42

The joyousness of Satan arriving on earth is as horrifying as the joy that 'sparkl'd in all thir eyes' when his mission was proposed in Hell.

At the beginning of Book IV there is yet another touch

that reveals the poet's intentness in imagining Satan's journey. Satan addresses the sun

> at whose sight all the Starrs
> Hide thir diminisht heads. [iv. 34–35

Having come from journeying among the stars Satan would be impressed by the unbroken sun-filled sky. It is one of those dramatic strokes that set the scene, and give interest and life to a narrative.

Now that Satan has reached his goal his eyes are unsealed and he realizes what he is about to attempt:

> To wreck on innocent frail man his loss
> Of that first Battel, and his flight to Hell. [iv.11–12

And he realises now what he has become:

> Now conscience wakes despair
> That slumberd, wakes the bitter memorie
> Of what he was, what is, and what must be
> Worse. [iv.23–26

Satan too suffers from a conscience but can only suffer: for him there is no way out of the pit of despair.

Constructionally the soliloquy that follows is accurately placed, for it brings into focus all that has happened and enables us to view it in true perspective. Satan has been presented in the first two Books in all his greatness; God has been presented in the first half of Book III: now comes the moment of truth, all the more irresistible because it is Satan who sees and reveals it. His soliloquy is a truly dramatic soliloquy; it consists not of words put into his mouth by the author but of words wrung from his soul in anguish. It is one of the crucial passages in the poem. Face to face with his ultimate objective it is natural that he should pause to reflect. So far he has been closely engaged with the difficulties and dangers of his journey to Earth; now at his journey's end he confronts God in his new creation. He sees

[126]

everything clearly, as in the light of the sun he begins by
addressing. What has been said before in Hell and Heaven
is recapitulated; but the arguments of Hell are now stated
without sophistry, the issues plainly put. It is self-revealing,
as a soliloquy should be. In Hell Satan had made a virtue of
pride and ambition, hatred and despair, with a confident air
that deluded himself and his followers, and still deludes
many readers. Now he admits that 'pride and worse ambition' were the causes of his original revolt; that it was a
revolt against the goodness of his Creator; that he was free
to stand or fall; that he is in consequence accurst; that there
is no way to salvation but by repentance and submission,
which he disdains. In short he finds after his flight that he is
still in Hell:

> Which way I flie is Hell; my self am Hell.   [iv. 75

This is the true comment on his earlier boast in Hell:

> The mind is its own place, and in it self
> Can make a Heav'n of Hell, a Hell of Heav'n.
> > [i. 254–5

(Most of Satan's most admired sayings have this same
dramatic irony.) In contrast to his own damnation behold
man and his newly created world: let us destroy it!

> So farewel Hope, and with Hope farewel Fear,
> Farewel Remorse: all Good to me is lost;
> Evil be thou my Good.   [iv. 108–10

Satan's heroism is defined in 'Evil be thou my Good'. Like
Macbeth, he recognizes his situation and does not relent.

Chapter 7

(i) ANGELS IN REVOLT

The war in Heaven is one of the episodes in the poem readers
are accustomed to write off as a total failure or a bad joke,
because it seems no more than an humourless attempt to
imitate Homeric battles. If we are to appreciate it at its true
value we must see, not only its satiric intent, but how it
answers the narrative conventions of the epic and also the
needs of the argument and story. By epic conventions I do
not mean merely the battles, which every epic in the classical
tradition must have, though this is a factor: I mean the function of the episode in the total structure of this particular
epic. The picture of monstrous disorder in the war in
Heaven is necessary to the total pattern of the poem – to
represent what has broken loose in Heaven with the revolt
of the angels, and to foreshadow what is to be, or may be,
let loose on earth, if Satan succeeds in his designs. It is a
supplement to the picture of disorder, ruin and violent evil
in the first two Books; only, this time with Adam's consciousness as centre of interest for the narrator. We have
been told of all this, and have seen the fallen angels in Hell;
Adam has not, and has no mental picture of what menaces
him and his world. It is also a part of the preparation for the
consequences of the human Fall: just as Sin and Death are
placed in readiness for their irruption into the human
universe when Satan begins his journey in Book II, so
they actually invade it as Satan returns to Hell in Book X.
The opening scenes in Hell, the war in Heaven and Satan's
return to Hell are set in counterpoise to the other parts of

the story. These are the narrative conventions of the epic to which I refer, the placing of theme against theme so that they illustrate and complete each other.

The episode is of further importance inasmuch as it affects our view of Satan. We heard at the outset that he had been overthrown by God but that tended only to heighten our admiration of his bearing and conduct in defeat; now we are to see him not only as the defeated leader but being defeated, to witness his ignominious fall. We see him now in his true colours, as God sees him. The reasons and motives for his revolt, specious when dramatically presented from his own point of view and amid the plaudits of his followers, are now seen in a different light as told by Raphael. Similarly in Book X we witness the ignominious conclusion of his triumphant return to Hell after accomplishing his mission on earth. It is not that the heroic figure of the earlier Books is deliberately degraded by the poet – an oft repeated but silly view – but that his mind and character are unfolded more and more fully by being seen in different circumstances and from different points of view.

Lastly, the war in Heaven is an opportunity for Milton's satire not only on epic battles but on war in general.

Raphael's account of the Fall of the angels proceeds from his telling Adam that the happiness of all God's creatures, in Heaven as on Earth, depends on their continuing obedience to God:

My self and all th' Angelic Host that stand
In sight of God enthron'd, our happie state
Hold, as you yours, while our obedience holds;
On other surety none; freely we serve
Because wee freely love, as in our will
To love or not; in this we stand or fall:
And som are fall'n, to disobedience fall'n,
And so from Heav'n to deepest Hell; O fall
From what high state of bliss into what woe!

[v. 535–43

[129]

He tells how before the world was made God in Heaven
declared his Son 'Messiah King', his vicegerent and lord
over all. Satan, 'fraught with envie',

> could not beare
> Through pride that sight, and thought himself impaird.
>
> [v. 664–5

Having drawn his legions apart he calls on them 'to cast off
this yoke'. He claims that in refusing to accept this new Lord
they are only asserting their right to equality and freedom.
And as usual he pretends to appeal to reason:

> Who can in reason then or right assume
> Monarchie over such as live by right
> His equals . . . ?
>
> [v. 794–6

In the event however he has to rely on the appeal not to
reason but to force.

Abdiel alone rejects these blasphemies and resists Satan:

> Shalt thou give Law to God, shalt thou dispute
> With him the points of libertie, who made
> Thee what thou art . . . ?
>
> [v. 822–4

To which Satan replies:

> Strange point and new!
> Doctrin which we would know whence learnt: who saw
> When this creation was? remembrest thou
> Thy making, while the Maker gave thee being?
> We know no time when we were not as now;
> Know none before us, self-begot, self-rais'd
> By our own quick'ning power, . . .
>
> [v. 855–61

Satan is trying to pull himself up by his own bootlaces. It
is the final blasphemy – the denial of his Maker and the
assertion of absolute, self-sufficient independence.

Commenting on the line describing Abdiel as

> Unshaken, unseduc't, unterrifi'd,
>
> [v. 899

Verity says 'Perhaps, when he wrote this line Milton had in mind his own position at the Restoration.' Again, when God commends Abdiel:

Servant of God, well don, well hast thou fought
The better fight, who single hast maintaind
Against revolted multitudes the Cause
Of Truth, in words mightier than they in Arms;
And for the testimonie of Truth hast borne
Universal reproach, far worse to bear
Than violence: for this was all thy care,
To stand approv'd in sight of God, though Worlds
Judg'd thee perverse.   [vi. 29–37

Verity asks, 'Is Milton here thinking of himself?' The answer in both instances is, 'No, he is thinking of Abdiel, and so should we be.' Abdiel is Milton's 'one just man', who reappears in the last two Books of the poem as well as in *Paradise Regain'd* and *Samson Agonistes*.

The war in Heaven in Book VI is usually regarded as Milton's serious attempt at an heroic battle, which had to be got in somewhere in an epic in the classical tradition; so regarded it cannot be defended against the criticism that 'this may be magnificent but it is not war'. A better view of the matter was given in an article by Arnold Stein in *E.L.H.*, September 1951, *Milton's War in Heaven – An Extended Metaphor*. An attentive reader, as he argues, must see that Milton is attempting something more complex and interesting than an imitation of the epic battle: the whole style and effect are not heroic but mock-heroic. This correctly indicates one of the motives of the war in Heaven as presented by Milton. Satan, as we have seen, is representative of the traditional epic hero, seeking glory by force of arms; one of Milton's aims therefore in the war in Heaven is to make Satan and his warriors look ridiculous. But the mockery goes beyond that, being aimed at warfare in general. It is all an extravagant satire on the belief in war as pre-eminently

E

heroic. The Book is filled with mockery: 'laughter was in
Heaven'. The mood is set by God's ironical words at the
outset, 'when smiling to his onely Son' he draws attention to
the rebellion hatching in the north. Milton's God always
regards and speaks of Satan's doings with the same contemptuous mockery; his sarcastic tone may not 'be pleasing
in a believer's ear' but it represents a perfectly reasonable
view of Satan's goings-on.

In the war of words that precedes the fighting Satan again
harps on his favourite theme of liberty against servitude:

> At first I thought that Libertie and Heav'n
> To heav'nly Soules had bin all one; but now
> I see that most through sloath had rather serve,
> Ministring Spirits, traind up in Feast and Song;
> Such hast thou armd, the Minstrelsie of Heav'n,
> Servilitie with freedom to contend,
> As both their deeds compar'd this day shall prove.
>
> [vi. 164–70

Through Satan Milton expresses scorn of his Heaven with
more wit than his critics can command. Abdiel's reply to
this taunt is important to an understanding of what follows:

> Unjustly thou deprav'st it with the name
> Of *Servitude* to serve whom God ordains
> Or Nature; God and Nature bid the same, . . .
>
> [vi. 174–6

This, which we have seen to be a central doctrine of
Milton's, provides another clue to his conduct of the war in
Heaven. The whole of nature, whether heavenly or human,
is God's creation and made from the same materials. It is
this that makes it possible for evil to originate in Heaven,
before it invades the Earth. When Michael confronts Satan
in the ensuing battle he says:

> Author of evil, unknown till thy revolt,
> . . . how hast thou disturbd

[132]

Heav'ns blessed peace, and into Nature brought
Miserie, uncreated till the crime
Of thy Rebellion !   [vi. 262–9

Because Heaven is a part of created nature, sin and misery
can invade it as they are to invade Paradise; only they are at
once purged from Heaven, and peace and order are quickly
restored. On Earth the contest between good and evil will
be prolonged through the ages; Earth is to be the main
scene of the conflict. Raphael's relation of the war in Heaven,
as he says, is for Adam's instruction, as being the origin and
parallel of the tragedy that might be re-enacted on Earth.

When, before the duel with Michael, Satan says,

The strife which thou callst evil, but wee style
The strife of Glorie: [vi. 289–90

he tells us once more how he, as opposed to the Satanists,
regards his own heroic role. When the two champions
change from words to blows the simile used to describe their
duel once again expresses the controlling idea that the revolt
of the angels has broken nature's order:

If Natures concord broke,
Among the Constellations warr were sprung,
Two Planets rushing from aspect malign
Of fiercest opposition in mid Skie,
Should combat, and thir jarring Sphears confound.
                                                      [vi. 311–15

This simile also prepares us for the very different character
of the second day's fighting.

Discussing the fortunes of the first day's fighting Satan
assures his companions that they have proved superior to
their enemies in all save the power of their weapons; what he
now proposes is that they should defeat God by turning the
forces of nature against their Creator. Since all things in
Heaven and Earth were created by God out of one first

[133]

matter, the glories of Heaven like those of Earth are built on 'dark foundations deep', are fashioned out of Chaos; and impious hands can rifle the bowels of heavenly as of earthly soil 'for Treasures better hid'. When Satan explains the infernal engines with which he hopes to overthrow their adversaries, he asks which of them who looks on the beauties of Heaven does not

> mind from whence they grow
> Deep under ground, materials dark and crude, . . .
> [vi. 477–8

The faithful angels for their part are also armed only with the forces of nature: the thunderbolt of God alone is supernatural. In short the two armies fight throughout on the physical plane:

> the least of whom could wield
> These Elements, and arm him with the force
> Of all thir Regions. [vi. 221–3

So the good angels answer the infernal artillery by hurling hills at their opponents. The battle, which had begun in seemingly serious epic style, now reaches its height of the extravagantly mock-heroic; it is Homeric epic comedy:

> Light as the Lightning glimpse they ran, they flew,
> From thir foundations loosning to and fro
> They pluckd the seated Hills with all thir load,
> Rocks, Waters, Woods, and by the shaggie tops
> Up lifting bore them in thir hands: Amaze,
> Be sure, and terror seiz'd the rebel Host,
> When coming towards them so dread they saw
> The bottom of the Mountains upward turnd,
> Till on those cursed Engins triple-row
> They saw them whelmd, and all thir confidence
> Under the weight of Mountains buried deep,
> Themselves invaded next, and on thir heads
> Main Promontories flung, which in the Air

Came shaddowing, and oppressd whole Legions armd. . . .
The rest in imitation to like Arms
Betook them, and the neighbouring Hills uptore;
So Hills amid the Air encounterd Hills
Hurld to and fro with jaculation dire,
That under ground they fought in dismal shade.

[vi. 642–66

This epic farce expresses Milton's opinion of war and its glories,

>Warrs hitherto the onely Argument
>Heroic deemd.

The answer to Johnson's criticism, mentioned in Chapter 2, that 'the confusion of spirit and matter' fills the whole narration with incongruity, will now be clear. Not only, says Johnson, are the rebel angels, 'now grown gross by sinning', crushed by their armour, but so are 'the uncorrupted angels, who were overthrown "the sooner for their arms, for unarmed they might easily as spirits have evaded by contraction or remove". . . . But if they could have escaped without their armour, they could have escaped from it and left only the empty cover to be battered.' This is good Johnsonian sense but he overlooks two points. A fight, even between angels, can only be conducted on the physical plane; Milton's philosophy, that there is no real distinction between the material and the spiritual, simply allows him to do this consistently and without demur. And there is the further point, that the ridiculous effects that result are deliberate; the fighting is intended as a parody, not only of epic battles but of warfare in general.

Destruction has now been pushed to the verge 'beyond which all Heav'n had gone to wrack'. The Father therefore sends forth his Son:

>Attended with ten thousand thousand Saints,
>He onward came, farr off his coming shon.

[vi. 767–8

Milton, as I have said, can express divine as well as Satanic energy. It is indeed easier to describe the give-and-take of battle, the effort of dangerous adventure, the fury of contention, than it is to render the effortless strength and energy of omnipotence. The remainder of the Book is one of the most triumphant passages in the poem, excelled only by the description in the next Book of the return of the Son to Heaven after the Creation. The verse moves straight on with uninterrupted power. The wrath of the Father, his terrible irresistible anger, is now seen in the 'mild Son':

> Stand still in bright array ye Saints, here stand
> Ye Angels armd, this day from Battel rest. . . .
>   So spake the Son, and into terror chang'd
> His count'nance too severe to be beheld
> And full of wrauth bent on his Enemies.
> . . . Full soon
> Among them he arriv'd. . . .
> . . . they astonisht all resistance lost,
> All courage; down thir idle weapons dropd;
> Ore Shields and Helms, and helmed heads he rode
> Of Thrones and mighty Seraphim prostrate,
> That wishd the Mountains now might be again
> Thrown on them as a shelter from his ire.
> Nor less on either side tempestuous fell
> His arrows, from the fourfold-visag'd Four
> Distinct with eyes, and from the living Wheels
> Distinct alike with multitude of eyes,
> One Spirit in them rul'd, and every eye
> Glar'd lightning, and shot forth pernicious fire
> Among th' accurst, that witherd all thir strength,
> And of thir wonted vigor left them draind,
> Exhausted, spiritless, afflicted, fall'n.
> Yet half his strength he put not forth, but checkd
> His Thunder in mid Vollie, for he meant
> Not to destroy, but root them out of Heav'n:
> The overthrown he rais'd, and as a Herd

Of Goats or timorous flock together throngd
Drove them before him Thunder-struck, persu'd
With terrors and with furies to the bounds
And Crystal wall of Heav'n, which op'ning wide
Rould inward, and a spacious Gap disclos'd
Into the wasteful Deep; the monstrous sight
Strook them with horror backward, but far worse
Urg'd them behind; headlong themselves they threw
Down from the verge of Heav'n, Eternal wrauth
Burnd after them to the bottomless pit.   [vi. 801–66

At this point the rebel angels approach nonentity. They are without will or sense of individual being, a mindless, panic-stricken rout. They who had boasted themselves 'self-begot' have temporarily ceased almost to be beings at all; they are as near to annihilation as living creatures can be.

We are now midway through the poem, and the narrative has returned to its starting point. The effect of Book VI is once again to put the two opening Books in proper perspective. We see the fallen angels now not from their own point of view but from God's. In Hell we were inclined to accept them at their own valuation; now we see them for what they are – great powers and immortal spirits, but powers and spirits of evil, who are helpless when God puts forth his might. We were shown their might and courage in the opening Books; now we are shown, not merely told, that they are as chaff before the wind when opposed to their Creator. The evil energy of Satan has collapsed before the divine energy of God. In the next Book we are to be shown the divine energy in the act not of destruction but of creation.

(ii) SATAN'S RETURN TO HELL

I now turn to Book X for the end of Satan's story, both because it will confirm what we have seen in Book VI and because we shall then be free to follow the central story of Adam and Eve uninterruptedly, when finally we come to it. After the Fall of man and the judgment pronounced on the three culprits by the Son in the Garden, the scene switches to Hell, where Sin and Death still sit within the open gates. We are back at the point where Satan set off on the mission now accomplished. What the poet is about to do is to show Hell and the powers of Hell for the last time in the poem, and to show them in all their loathsomeness and horror and ultimate futility, stripped of the glamour of heroism and romance, the dignity and pathos, with which they were invested in the opening Books. The colloquy between Sin and Death, sitting 'in counterview' within the gates, is as horrible as anything in literature. By 'a wondrous sympathy' they divine Satan's success in the new world of man, and themselves prepare to invade it. Sin describes this instinctive knowledge in words that remind us of the first intoxicating effects of the forbidden fruit on Adam and Eve:

> Methinks I feel new strength within me rise,
> Wings growing and Dominion giv'n me large
> Beyond this Deep.   [x. 243–5

Death too is sentient of his coming prey:

> with delight he snuffd the smell
> Of mortal change on Earth. . . .
> So scented the grim Feature, and upturnd
> His Nostril wide into the murkie Air,
> Sagacious of his Quarry from so farr.
>   [x. 272–81

The vague 'grim Feature' (i.e. 'Shape') followed by the

definite 'Nostril wide' is an excellent example of how Milton manages to depict these shadowy figures.

In building their bridge over Chaos, Sin and Death, as Till-yard has observed (*S.P.*, XXXVIII), 'parody God's creative act in the seventh book'; they 'hover over the waters of Chaos (birds of prey, not the dove); . . . and instead of warmth they infuse cold and petrifaction'. The extended description of the bridging of Chaos, with its frequent similes, is one of those imaginative and verbal feats we come to take for granted in Milton. And this tremendous emblem of the cosmic consequences of the Fall seems to have been Milton's invention:

> a ridge of pendent Rock
> Over the vext Abyss, following the track
> Of *Satan*, to the self same place where hee
> First lighted from his Wing, and landed safe
> From out of *Chaos* to the outside bare
> Of this round World: . . .
> . . . and now in little space
> The confines met of Empyrean Heav'n
> And of this World, and on the left hand Hell
> With long reach interpos'd; three sev'ral ways
> In sight, to each of these three places led.
>
> [x. 313–24

As Sin and Death look down on Earth they see Satan flying towards them: 'Great joy was at thir meeting'. This meeting of the unholy trinity is one of the great junctures of the poem. As Satan stands admiring the 'stupendious Bridge' the exchanges between him and his daughter parody again the relation of the heavenly Father and Son:

> O Parent, these are thy magnific deeds, . . .
> Thou art thir Author and prime Architect.
>
> [x. 354–6

To which Satan replies that his offspring have 'amply merited' of him. At this moment Satan·is indeed standing on the top of the world. He now sends Sin and Death on their way to Paradise:

> they with speed
> Thir course through thickest Constellations held
> Spreading thir bane.   [x. 410–12

It has always been held that Sin and Death, as allegories, should not be actors in the story. Addison says, 'I cannot think that Persons of such a Chymerical Existence are proper actors in an Epick poem. . . . Virgil has, indeed, admitted Fame as an Actress in the *Aeneid*, but the part she acts is very short.' Johnson objects that they are a confusion of the real and the ideal, similar in kind to the confusion of the material and immaterial in the war in Heaven: 'Sin is indeed the mother of Death and may be allowed to be the portress of Hell; but when they stop the journey of Satan, a journey described as real, and when Death offers him battle, the allegory is broken. That Sin and Death might have shewn the way to Hell might have been allowed; but they cannot facilitate the passage by building a bridge, because the difficulty of Satan's passage is described as real and sensible, and the bridge ought to be only figurative. . . . Sin and Death worked up a "mole of aggregated soil", cemented with asphaltus; a work too bulky for ideal architects.'

These criticisms have been generally accepted as valid. Yet Milton's Sin and Death are not allegory in the sense of being 'a continued allegory and darke conceit'; they are personifications who play obvious and appropriate parts in the story. As for their being chimerical and fictitious they were in fact as real to people of the time as Satan himself, not only as representing two inescapable conditions of life, but from their representation in painting and sculpture, in sermon, drama and literature generally. And since Sin and Death are a main part of the argument Milton could hardly do other than make them characters in his mythology. They must therefore be shown in action, just as Satan must; in an epic treatment of the Fall it is not enough to show their presence merely through their effects on nature and in the consciousness of man. The reverse of what Johnson says is the truth of the matter: it is only in so far as these ideal characters and their doings are real and sensible that they are convincing and effective.

Helen Darbishire, in her James Bryce Memorial Lecture on *Paradise Lost*, argued that Johnson put his finger on the wrong place in his criticism of Milton's handling of these figures: 'The real clash comes in Milton's story when the *persons* Sin and Death come into collision with the inner conception which they represent, and this must inevitably happen when they reach Paradise and approach Adam and Eve. Sin as a state of being became a part of their consciousness the moment they ate the apple: Death as a further state of being entered their minds after their sin was completed. But the personified characters, Sin and Death, Satan's repellent and disreputable relatives, arrive *afterwards* in Paradise; and then the trouble begins. Milton with his acutely logical mind is fully conscious of this collision between two modes of conception.' She then quotes these lines as far as 'in body':

> Mean while in Paradise the hellish pair
> Too soon arriv'd, *Sin* there in power before,
> Once actual, now in body, and to dwell
> Habitual habitant.   [x. 585–8

Helen Darbishire overlooked the fact that Milton's mind is not only acutely logical but nicely theological, and so misses the double meanings in these verses. They must be read in the light of the passage in Chapter IX of *The Christian Doctrine* on the subject of the three stages of sin in Paradise: first, potential sin or 'the liability to fall with which man was created'; secondly, 'what is called actual sin', that is the first act of sin by our first parents, which

[141]

Milton agrees with some other theologians in distinguishing from 'original sin'; thirdly, original sin, 'the evil concupiscence' which our first parents 'transmitted to their posterity . . . in the shape of an innate propensity to sin. This is called in Scripture "the old man" and "the body of sin", Rom. vi. 6, Eph. iv. 22.' The theological meaning of the verses therefore is that sin was potentially in Paradise from the beginning, was actually there with the first act of disobedience, and finally was there in the consequent lust of Adam and Eve, the carnal desires with which all their posterity would be afflicted. There is no conflict between these concepts of sin and the *person* Sin.

Then there is Miss Darbishire's example of the clash between the *person* Death and the conception he represents: 'Eve's idea of Death as a person intrudes upon Adam's metaphysical questionings of what the state of death really means.

> Let us seek Death [she suggests] or he not found, supply
> With our own hands his office on ourselves.
>
> [x. 1001–2

That is, let us seek Death, or if we can't find Death, let's die.' This is to misconstrue in order to make a point: Eve says, not 'let's die' but 'let's kill ourselves'. There is a difference between suffering death and committing suicide. As yet Adam and Eve know nothing of death except that it is the end of life; they are ignorant of what form it will take, or who will be the agent. When Adam is later shown the vision of Cain killing Abel he says,

> But have I now seen Death? Is this the way
> I must return to dust? [xi. 462–3

In the circumstances it is not unnatural that Eve should think of Death as a person to be encountered, or that she should suppose that either he or they themselves might be the executioners.

[142]

It must be admitted that these shadowy figures (sublime, as Burke observed, by their very obscurity) are always in danger of becoming too definite in their actions, something more than pervasive powers. This does not happen at the places cited; to my sense there is only one place where it does, which is when Satan and Death at their first meeting challenge each other to mortal combat. We are told,

> and now great deeds
> Had been achiev'd, whereof all Hell had rung,
> [ii. 722–3

had not Sin intervened to save the situation. But one fails to imagine – and doubts whether even Milton could have imagined – what possible issue there could be to a fight between two such combatants. This one instance is enough to show what control was necessary to avoid similar absurdities elsewhere. The use of these personifications as characters in the action was a bold stroke, but the whole story demanded such boldness; and the Miltonic sublimity in presenting them is the measure of his success in meeting these demands of the story.

To return to Satan, who meanwhile has gone down 'the Causey to Hell Gate'. He stages his re-entry into Pandaemonium with all his customary histrionic art. What follows is a masterpiece of dramatic irony. He passes unnoticed through the watching legions, in the disguise of a common soldier; and then assumes invisibility as he enters the council chamber and ascends

> his high Throne, which under state
> Of richest texture spred, at th' upper end
> Was plac't in regal lustre.   [x. 445–7

We are back in imagination at the opening of Book II:

> High on a Throne of Royal State . . .
> *Satan* exalted sat.   [ii. 1–5

[143]

For the last time we see the Satan of the earlier Books, in all his power and glory. He savours his coming triumph before revealing himself:

> Down a while
> He sate, and round about him saw unseen:
> At last as from a Cloud his fulgent head
> And shape Starr-bright appear'd, . . .   [x. 447–50

It is a memorable picture, full of character and of meaning. We are meant to recall the passages in which the invisible God is described as enthroned in a cloud of light. As Satan's 'great consulting Peers' come forward acclaiming him he stills them with a motion of his hand, and begins to address them with that superb apostrophe,

> Thrones, Dominations, Princedoms, Vertues, Powers,
>   [x. 460

first used by God when declaring the exaltation of his Only Son to lordship over the assembled angels, and repeated by Satan soon afterwards when suggesting to his legions that these magnific titles have become merely titular since all power was delegated by the Father to the Son. Now, he tells them, he has restored reality to their titles by putting them in possession of

> a spacious World, to our native Heaven
> Little inferior.   [x. 467–8

There is grim irony in Satan's words when, unaware of the changes wrought by his victory, he speaks of this new world as being 'of absolute perfection'. He ends his speech:

> What remains, ye Gods,
> But up and enter now into full bliss.
>   So having said, a while he stood, expecting
> Thir universal shout and high applause
> To fill his ear, when contrary he hears

On all sides, from innumerable tongues
A dismal universal hiss, the sound
Of public scorn; he wonderd, but not long
Had leasure, wondring at himself now more.
[x. 502–10

The transformation of Satan and his fallen angels into writhing, frustrated snakes is deplored and resented by some readers as a violent and unjustifiable degradation of these splendid beings; of Satan especially it is said that there is no relation between the earlier noble figure and this 'monstrous Serpent on his Belly prone'. This, however, is simply a question of whether one has been willing to see the devils as the poet sees them and has presented them: his view of them has not varied, though the point of view from which they are presented has varied with the turns of the story. His very words in treating this last episode show, as I have noted, that he had clearly in mind the earlier, more comely picture of them. And this reminiscence comes again unmistakably in describing these swarming reptiles:

dreadful was the din
Of hissing through the Hall, thick swarming now
With complicated monsters, head and tail, . . .
[x. 521–3

The words recall an earlier transformation at the first entry of the devils into this same hall:

Thick swarmd, both on the ground and in the air,
Brusht with the hiss of russling wings. As Bees
In spring time, . . .   [i. 767–9

Bees may be more pleasant than snakes but the poet can hold both images in his mind as representing his devils at two different points in the story. We have come a long way and have had occasion to modify our first impressions of the fallen angels; if we have refused to allow our impressions

[145]

to be modified, that is not the poet's fault – he has done his part. He has reached the end of the story of Satan and his associates in the poem – we are to see no more of them, though Satan and his ultimate doom will be briefly described – and now is the time to show them as they really are. The poet must now express all his hatred and scorn of them; this is no time for sympathy but for pitiless judgement. Their loathsomeness must now be portrayed as were their earlier, more attractive phases.

Chapter 8

THE CREATION

Raphael tells of the creation of the human universe in answer to Adam's

> desire to know
> What nearer might concern him, how this World
> Of Heav'n and Earth conspicuous first began, . . .
> [vii. 61–63

God declares his purpose to create a new world of men to repair the loss to Heaven of the fallen angels:

> till by degrees of merit rais'd
> They open to themselves at length the way
> Up hither, under long obedience tri'd,
> And Earth be chang'd to Heav'n, and Heav'n to Earth,
> One Kingdom, Joy and Union without end.
> [vii. 157–61

The description of the Son issuing from the gates of Heaven and riding into Chaos on his mission of creation is set in deliberate contrast to that of Satan issuing from the gates of Hell on his mission of destruction. Here is the earlier passage:

> on a sudden open flie
> With impetuous recoil and jarring sound
> Th' infernal dores, and on thir hinges grate
> Harsh Thunder, that the lowest bottom shook
> Of *Erebus*. . . .
> Before thir eyes in sudden view appear
> The secrets of the hoarie Deep, a dark
> Illimitable Ocean without bound, . . .

Into this wild Abyss the warie Fiend
Stood on the brink of Hell and lookd a while,
Pondering his Voyage, for no narrow frith
He had to cross.   [ii. 879–920

There follows the episode of Satan battling his 'uncouth
way' through Chaos. Against this picture of strenuous
heroism is now set the picture of omnipotence in action,
calm and irresistible:

                        Heav'n opend wide
    Her ever during Gates, Harmonious sound
    On golden Hinges moving, to let forth
    The King of Glorie in his powerful Word
    And Spirit coming to create new Worlds.
    On heav'nly ground they stood, and from the shore
    They viewd the vast immeasurable Abyss
    Outrageous as a Sea, dark, wasteful, wild,
    Up from the bottom turnd by furious winds
    And surging waves, as Mountains to assault
    Heav'ns highth, and with the Center mix the Pole.
        Silence, ye troubl'd waves, and thou Deep, peace,
    Said then th' Omnific Word, your discord end:
        Nor stayd, but on the Wings of Cherubim
    Uplifted, in Paternal Glorie rode
    Farr into *Chaos*, and the World unborn;
    For *Chaos* heard his voice: him all his Traine
    Followd in bright procession to behold
    Creation, and the wonders of his might. [vii. 205–23

The following account of the Creation is one of Milton's
supreme poetical feats. Even after the event one's imagination boggles at the thought of any poet attempting what he
has succeeded in doing in this seventh Book. With a few
verses of Genesis as his text, and those few among the
sublimest in literature, he undertakes to write out in full
epic manner this story of the Creation. It calls for all his
learning in natural history, but learning of course supplied.

[148]

no more than the crude materials for the task. The living wonder of creation must be displayed and must live in every word. The poetic exaltation must be sustained throughout, not only in describing the sublimities of the creation of light, of the separation of the firmament, of the emergence of the land from the sea, of the glories of the sun and moon and stars, but also in the long catalogue of living creatures down to the very humblest; and the mention of each particular creature and plant must thrill with the marvel of creation and the excitement of life first seen. The total effect depends on the accumulation of lively detail, and a long quotation is needed to illustrate it. I quote from the paragraph describing the creation of fishes and birds:

Forthwith the Sounds and Seas, each Creek and Bay
With Frie innumerable swarm, and Shoals
Of Fish that with thir Finns and shining Scales
Glide under the green Wave, in Sculls that oft
Bank the mid Sea: part single or with mate
Graze the Sea weed thir pasture, and through Groves
Of Coral stray, or sporting with quick glance
Show to the sun thir wav'd coats dropt with Gold,
Or in thir Pearlie shells at ease, attend
Moist nutriment, or under Rocks thir food
In jointed Armour watch: on smooth the Seal
And bended Dolphins play: part huge of bulk
Wallowing unwieldie, enormous in thir Gait
Tempest the Ocean: . . . .
Mean while the tepid Caves, and Fens and Shores
Thir brood as numerous hatch, from th' Egg that soon
Bursting with kindly rupture forth disclos'd
Thir callow young, but featherd soon, and fledge
They summd thir Penns, and soaring th' air sublime
With clang despis'd the ground, under a cloud
In prospect; there the Eagle and the Stork
On Cliffs and Cedar tops thir Eyries build:
Part loosely wing the Region, part more wise

In common, rang'd in figure wedge thir way,
Intelligent of seasons, and set forth
Thir Aerie Caravan high over Seas
Flying, and over Lands with mutual wing
Easing thir flight; so steers the prudent Crane
Her annual Voyage, borne on Winds; the Aire
Floats, as they pass, fanned with unnumberd plumes:
From Branch to Branch the smaller Birds with song
Solac'd the Woods, and spred thir painted wings
Till Ev'n, nor then the solemn Nightingal
Ceas'd warbling, but all night tun'd her soft lays:
Others on Silver Lakes and Rivers Bath'd
Thir downie Brest; the Swan with Arched neck
Between her white wings mantling proudly, Rows
Her state with Oarie feet: yet oft they quit
The Dank, and rising on swift Pennons, tour
The mid Aëreal Skie: Others on ground
Walkd firm; the crested Cock whose clarion sounds
The silent hours, and th' other whose gay Train
Adorns him, colourd with the Florid hue
Of Rainbows and Starrie Eyes.   [vii. 399–446

Such sustained description is not informed by booklearning alone; these things must have been seen and felt, 'felt in the blood, and felt along the heart'. Here is the marvel of nature, each general description with its enlivening touches and apt words. Here is Milton in his old age still the lover of nature, still seeing it vividly in his mind's eye, and still glorying in it as a manifestation of God's goodness and power. Landor, answering Dryden's criticism that Milton 'saw Nature through the spectacles of Books', says: 'Unhappily . . . Dryden saw Nature from between the houses of Fleet Street. If ever there was a poet who knew her well, and described her in all her loveliness, it was Milton.'

This whole Book is a rapturous song to the Creation, and the verse reaches its triumphant climax in the ascent of the Son from his completed work:

[150]

Up he rode
Followd with acclamation and the sound
Symphonious of ten thousand Harpes that tun'd
Angelic harmonies: the Earth, the Aire
Resounded, (thou rememberst for thou heardst)
The Heav'ns and all the Constellations rung,
The Planets in thir station list'ning stood,
While the bright Pomp ascended jubilant.
Open, ye everlasting Gates, they sung,
Open, ye Heav'ns, your living dores; let in
The Great Creator from his work returnd
Magnificent, his Six days work, a World.

[vii. 557–68

The total effect of this Book (and this is a chief part of its importance in the action) is that we now realize the beauty and grandeur (and what we may have doubted before) the excitement of this new life of man, the glory of his destiny, and all that depends on Adam's faithfulness. Another point in regard to the construction, as Tillyard observed, is that in the course of the Book we have been brought back to Earth. We realize what has happened when at the beginning of the next Book Adam puts his astronomical inquiries to Raphael and we find ourselves 'standing on Earth' and looking away from it to the stars.

When Adam starts his astronomical inquiries Eve prudently retires from the scene:

With lowliness Majestic from her seat,
And Grace that won who saw to wish her stay,
Rose, and went forth among her Fruits and Flowrs, . . .
With Goddess-like demeanour forth she went.

[viii. 42–59

How well Milton describes movement of any kind! The poet takes care to impress the figure of Eve on our imaginations as she departs because the discussion on sexual love that follows the discussion on astronomy is to centre on her.

[151]

This is indeed the narrator's real reason for dismissing her at
this point. The reason imputed to her by the poet is that,
although not uninterested in or incapable of understanding
the abstruse matters that Raphael and Adam are about to em-
bark on, she prefers to hear of them from her husband, 'Adam
relating, she sole Auditress'; but this is not the real reason,
only the story-teller's way of covering up. The real reason
appears later, when Adam comes to tell Raphael of Eve's
creation, of their nuptials and of the effect of her beauty on
him; it would have been psychologically impossible for
Adam to tell of these things, and to carry on the discussion
with Raphael on sexual love, in Eve's presence; and impossible for her to be there without offending against
modesty. Such provision for coming events is another
instance of Milton's narrative craft.

The discussion on the Ptolemaic and Copernican theories,
on whether the sun goes round the earth or the earth round
the sun, is not dragged in to 'salve Milton's conscience', or to
show that his astronomical knowledge was up-to-date. It was
a central theological question of the time and therefore
germane to Milton's theme; and that is how Raphael treats
it, glad of this further opportunity to instruct Adam whilst
satisfying his doubts of why God made this immense universe as a setting to the tiny earth, and why the heavens with
their sun and moon and numberless stars should revolve
through incomprehensible distances and at unimaginable
speeds

> merely to officiate light
> Round this opacous Earth, this punctual spot, . . .
> [viii. 22–23

In the end Raphael advises him to

> be lowlie wise:
> Think onely what concernes thee and thy being.
> [viii. 173–4

This is still good sense, despite our proud scientific learning. Ultimately it is a moral question, as we are coming
more and more to perceive.

There are verses in the course of this exposition that show
how Milton can make poetry of these matters, as Sylvester
in his translation of Du Bartas, from which Milton lifts a
phrase here and there, cannot:

> Whether the Sun predominant in Heav'n
> Rise on the Earth, or Earth rise on the Sun,
> Hee from the East his flaming road begin,
> Or Shee from West her silent course advance
> With inoffensive pace that spinning sleeps
> On her soft Axle, while she paces ev'n
> And bears thee soft with the smooth Air along, . . .
>   [viii. 160–6

The imaginative apprehension of

> With inoffensive pace that spinning sleeps

is the equal of Marlowe's

> All things that move between the quiet Poles.

Chapter 9

PARADISE

I come now to the central story of Adam and Eve. The story of the Fall was as difficult and unpromising a subject as was ever chosen by a narrative poet. What has to be shown is man and woman in their primal state of innocence falling into sin through the wiles of a serpent. As simply told in a few verses of Genesis we accept it easily enough, one way or another; but can such a story be written out large in epic form without becoming absurd and incredible? It would seem an impossible task. Yet if *Paradise Lost* fails here at its centre it fails altogether; all the strength of imagination in displaying the surrounding drama of Heaven and Hell and the Creation, all the magnificence of the writing, will have gone to waste. A. J. A. Waldock in *'Paradise Lost' and its Critics* (1947), argued that it did so fail, and since he represents a modern school of Milton criticism I shall use him as devil's advocate in an attempt to justify the poet.

Waldock protested against the tendency in recent criticism of *Paradise Lost* to concentrate on the meaning of the poem, and to interpret the story in the light of that meaning. He himself would have us go to the other extreme and look simply at the truth of the story as it affects the modern reader: 'It is our impressions of the story as it is told that constitute the facts of the poem; . . . . Between the impressions of natural, easygoing, unprejudiced readers there is, I believe, no great variation. Differences mount with sophistication – because the registering mind, so to say, comes to know too much. What happens is that our unforced sense of what is occurring is often complicated . . . by what Milton expects us to think is occurring. We know what he expects, partly from the information we bring to the poem, partly from prods and reminders that Milton administers to us within it. . . . Unless we recognize that within the poem itself presentation and commentary may clash, we can make little headway . . . towards the truth about *Paradise Lost*.'

The suppressed assumption in Waldock's argument is that we need take no account of differences in conventions of thought and feeling between the seventeenth century and our own; for his 'natural, easygoing, unprejudiced readers' are obviously ignorant and careless of such differences. Now such readers, far from being unprejudiced, will substitute their own prejudices, their own modern conventions of thought and feeling, for Milton's; that, as we shall see, is what Waldock himself does. The clash of which he speaks is a clash between these prejudices, not between Milton's story and its meaning. The contrary view I shall be arguing is that Milton's telling of his story is controlled by ideas many of which, though common enough then and readily understood, are not only not common now but are even contrary to our ruling ideas. Before we can judge whether the poet has successfully presented those ideas through the story (and I agree that the success of the story is the criterion) we must first understand and for the time being accept them.

The story starts in Book IV with our introduction to Paradise and its inhabitants in their original state of nature. As was said in Chapter 2, this state is one in which man and his world are ruled by inherent goodness, by a law of natural obedience to God's will. In the mind of man this law of nature is conscious and is called 'reason' or 'right reason'. How then in this state of natural goodness can evil enter to corrupt man and his world? The story-teller relies on the doctrine of Free Will and on the fact that Satan is free to 'attempt the mind of Man'. We first enter Paradise with Satan; it is in his presence, and partly through his eyes, that we first see Adam and Eve in their state of innocence. Evil has already entered Paradise to threaten that state. But it is only by deceiving man's reason that Satan can succeed in his purpose; as Adam says to Eve, they are 'secure from outward force'.

Adam and Eve are presented as happy lovers in this state of natural goodness. Their mutual love, in relation to their loving obedience to God, on which it depends, is the key to the harmony of their world. This is the central theme of their story, symbolized by the recurrent phrase 'hand in hand'. Through Adam and Eve in Paradise Milton depicts his ideal of wedded love. It is the same ideal as Spenser had portrayed in Book III of *The Faerie Queene,* a natural sexual love that is also chaste. In the *Doctrine and Discipline of Divorce,* as we have seen, Milton had insisted that the chief and noblest end of marriage is 'not the nuptial bed' but 'a meet and happy conversation', that is to say a social, intellectual and spiritual, not merely a physical intercourse. This is the ideal depicted in *Paradise Lost* also, but here the emphasis is different in response to the needs of the story: here he insists on the sexuality of Adam and Eve, though in such a way as to set off and enhance its 'simplicitie and spotless innocence':

> So passd they naked on, nor shunnd the sight
> Of God or Angel, for they thought no ill:
> So hand in hand they passd, the lovliest pair
> That ever since in loves imbraces met, . . .
> [iv. 319–22

There is no more thrilling love poetry in the language than is to be found in all the Books of *Paradise Lost* in which Adam and Eve figure; and it is a love poetry of many

[156]

moods. One of the more astonishing vagaries of general literary opinion is that expressed by Grierson in his Introduction to *Donne's Poetical Works*: 'Milton never wrote any English love-poetry, unless it be the one sonnet on the death of the wife who might have opened the sealed wells of his heart.' This failure even to notice the continual passages of great love poetry in *Paradise Lost* is due primarily, as Grierson's words suggest, to the inveterate belief since Johnson's *Life* that Milton the man was incapable of tenderness, especially towards the other sex. For many readers of the poem this belief is borne out by Milton's view of the relationship of the sexes:

> Hee for God onely, Shee for God in him. [iv. 299

On which Eve's words are the best gloss:

> My Author and Disposer, what thou bidst
> Unargu'd I obey; so God ordains,
> God is thy Law; thou mine. [iv. 635–7

('Disposer' here means 'ruler'). This again I have previously demonstrated to be the Pauline doctrine that had always been taught by the Church and was a commonplace not seriously questioned by anyone in the seventeenth century. A view with so long an history, and not only in Christendom, cannot be dismissed as eccentric or perverse. Nor has it ever proved incompatible with the writing of love poetry. So it is that Eve's words of complete submission to Adam lead on to the exquisite declaration of love for him as the source of all her happiness and delight in the world:

> With thee conversing I forget all time,
> All seasons and thir change, all please alike.

The view of woman's subordinate place is seen in perspective when put alongside the opposing romantic view, deriving from the medieval literature of chivalric or courtly love, which reversed the relations of the sexes and exalted woman as the object of man's devotion and worship. This revolutionary idea, which would have appeared as strange to the ancient pagan world as to St. Paul, has dominated European love literature since its introduction in the troubadour poetry of the twelfth century; even today, unromantic as we like to think ourselves, there is no difficulty in understanding and appreciating it. Courtly love was based on the analogy of the feudal relationship: as the vassal obeyed and served his lord so the lover obeyed and served his lady. She is his superior by virtue of her sex, her beauty and her goodness; and she inspires him to all worthy sentiments, thoughts and deeds. Sexual love is proclaimed as, in C. S. Lewis's words, 'a noble and ennobling passion'. In a religious age this exaltation of woman and of the sexual passion becomes a religion of love, in conscious opposition to Christianity; most love poetry from the twelfth to the seventeenth century, in one way or another, shows an awareness of this conflict between human and divine love. Milton too believes that human love can be noble and ennobling, but not by the adoration of woman or by submission of the mind to the passion of love. He agrees with the theologians that the subjugation of the reason by passion is evil, and that sexual life before the Fall was innocent because the mind did not then surrender its sovereignty to the passion of love. Aquinas, arguing this thesis, goes so far as to claim that all sensual pleasures before the Fall were not lessened but heightened by being controlled by the reason; 'as a sober person does not take less pleasure in food taken in moderation than the glutton'. Most of us are not likely to be convinced of the reality of such a delectable existence by the cold logic of the theologian; only a poet can enable us to imagine it. One remembers that Milton had done so when he made even the licentious Comus experience the keenness of this chaste, rational pleasure as he listened to the Lady singing:

Such sober certainty of waking bliss
I never heard till now.

These then are the chief ideas Milton works with. To turn now to the story in which they are enacted. As soon as he has introduced us to Adam and Eve in Paradise Milton prepares the way, with a story-teller's prudence, for the climax of the Fall. The state of innocence in Paradise cannot of itself, or without an effect of psychological and aesthetic violence, give rise to sin and tragedy. Something therefore must happen, something more than the mere presence of Satan, to make us conscious of man's frailty, of the precariousness of his situation, of the possibility of evil entering to corrupt him and his world; some premonition of coming events. This must happen at once, since Satan disappears from the scene at the end of Book IV and does not reappear in the Garden until the climax of the story in Book IX; the intervening four Books are occupied with Raphael's visit, and include the episode of the War in Heaven and the Creation. With so long a stretch of intervening narrative it is essential that before he departs Satan should demonstrate his power as the Tempter, in order to promote and keep the tension of the story. Yet nothing must be done at this point to interrupt the peace of Paradise or to call in question its state of perfection. It is a nice problem in story-telling, and it is nicely solved.

Satan, listening to the talk of Adam and Eve, has learned that the fruit of the Tree of Knowledge of Good and Evil is forbidden them, as sole pledge of their obedience to God; the same night he acts on this hint. He is found by the Guardian Angels

Squat like a Toad, close at the ear of *Eve*,   [iv. 800

inspiring her with an evil dream. The dream, as wonderingly related by Eve to Adam next morning, begins with her hearing a voice, which she thinks to be Adam's, calling her forth to walk in the moonlight – this, as Adam later remarks, reflects their talk of the previous evening. She goes in search of him and suddenly finds herself before the Tree of Knowledge. Beside the tree stands an angel, who scoffs at God's envious interdiction of knowledge. He himself then eats of the fruit and offers it to Eve:

> Taste this, and be henceforth among the Gods
> Thy self a Goddess, not to Earth confin'd.
> . . . the pleasant savourie smell
> So quickend appetite, that I, methought,
> Could not but taste. Forthwith up to the Clouds
> With him I flew, and underneath beheld
> The Earth outstretcht immense, a prospect wide
> And various: wondring at my flight and change
> To this high exaltation: suddenly
> My Guide was gon, and I, me thought, sunk down,
> And fell asleep; but O how glad I wak'd
> To find this but a dream!   [v. 77–93

This is a good example of Milton's narrative skill, every touch right. As a rehearsal of her actual temptation and fall, the dream would put ideas into Eve's head, unconsciously prompting her later actions and weakening her resistance. It is a psychological conditioning for her fall.

Adam is as perturbed as Eve by this 'uncouth dream' but comforts her and himself with the thought that

> Evil into the mind of God or Man
> May come and go, so unapprov'd, and leave
> No spot or blame behind.   [v. 117–19

In 'The Crisis of *Paradise Lost*' (*Studies in Milton*, 1951,) Tillyard argued that while in the abstract this doctrine may be tenable, the effect of the incident, 'its dramatic truth', is that 'Eve has really passed from innocence to sin', that her fall has already taken place. But this is to refuse to go along with the poet in the telling of his story, indeed to lay down conditions that would make it a story impossible to tell. Sin is an act, and must be conscious and willing. What we have been shown is Eve's liability to temptation; but she has not been shown as sinning in thought or deed, and we can continue to think of her as innocent. The dream, though ominous, is a passing ripple on the serene surface of life in Paradise.

Whereas Eve is to be tempted by Satan, Adam is to be tempted by Eve. This too the poet must prepare for and he does so in the second half of Book VIII, which provides the next stage in the story. Tillyard argued that at this point in turn we witness Adam's virtual fall; but once more all we are shown is Adam's liability to sin, a necessary postulate of the story.

After their discussion on astronomy in the beginning of Book VIII Adam proceeds to tell Raphael of his first moments of conscious life, describing his joy in being alive and his wondering delight in the world about him:

> Thou Sun, said I, fair Light,
> And thou enlightend Earth, so fresh and gay,
> Ye Hills and Dales, ye Rivers, Woods and Plains,
> And ye that live and move, fair Creatures, tell,
> Tell, if ye saw, how came I thus, how here?
> Not of my self; by some great Maker then,
> In goodness and in power præeminent;
> From whom I have that thus I move and live,
> And feel that I am happier than I know.
>
> [viii. 273–82

Here we see the effect of Book VII, the joy of the Creation, coming into the central human story. It is easy enough to laugh at this or that incident in Milton's Paradise, and there is no great harm in indulging one's mirth so long as it does not become smug and vulgar, and prevent one seeing the poetic fact here realized: 'Bliss was it in that dawn to be alive.'

[161]

After telling of his own creation Adam next tells of his talk with God about his solitary state and of the creation of Eve. And it is now that the poet begins to prepare the ground for his treatment of Adam's fall:

> Under his forming hands a Creature grew,
> Manlike, but different Sex, so lovely faire
> That what seemd fair in all the World, seemd now
> Mean, or in her summd up, in her containd
> And in her looks, which from that time infus'd
> Sweetness into my heart, unfelt before,
> And into all things from her Air inspir'd
> The spirit of love and amorous delight.   [viii. 470–7

He goes on to speak of the strange disturbing power of Eve's beauty. His senses find delight in all around him, but only in her presence does he feel such delight as overcomes him:

>   transported I behold,
> Transported touch; here passion first I felt,
> Commotion strange, in all enjoyments else
> Superior and unmov'd, here onely weake
> Against the charm of Beautys powerful glance.
>   [viii. 529–33

'Charm', as used here of feminine beauty and again at the climax of the story, has lost its original force. In Milton's time the primary meaning was still 'a magic spell; a mysterious, extraordinary or preternatural power to influence, subdue, control'. What Adam is saying is that the power of Eve's beauty seems preternatural in subduing his reason by passion; it is contrary to nature – using 'nature' in the sense already explained:

> For well I understand in the prime end
> Of Nature her th' inferior, in the mind
> And inward Faculties, which most excell,
> ....; yet when I approach

Her loveliness, so absolute she seems
And in her self complete, so well to know
Her own, that what she wills to do or say
Seems wisest, vertuousest, discreetest, best;
All higher knowledge in her presence falls
Degraded, Wisdom in discourse with her
Loses discount'nanc't, and like folly shews;
Autority and Reason on her wait,
As one intended first, not after made
Occasionally; and to consummat all,
Greatness of mind and nobleness thir seat
Build in her loveliest, and create an awe
About her, as a guard Angelic plac't.   [viii. 540–59

Waldock calls this speech a curious mixture: 'At one
moment he merely mouths his author's theories of woman's
place and function. . . . At another, his tribute is so deep
and moving that one can hardly relate it to the tone with
which he seemed to begin.' Waldock did not seem to
realize that he too was relying on theories of woman's place
and function, only they are different from Milton's. If we
accept the poet's view of woman's place and function there is
nothing inconsistent or unnatural in the progression of
Adam's thought. He begins by wondering at the excessive
power of sexual love, beyond nature and reason; he ends by
acknowledging the effect it creates of Eve's intellectual and
moral superiority – a glorious expression of romantic love,
which Waldock approves but Raphael does not. Raphael
admonishes Adam not to yield to this illusion of passion,
coolly pointing out its basis in physical passion:

Accuse not Nature, she hath don her part;
Do thou but thine, and be not diffident
Of Wisdom, . . .
For what admir'st thou, what transports thee so,
An outside? fair no doubt, and worthy well
Thy cherishing, thy honouring, and thy love,
Not thy subjection: . . .

F   [163]

What higher in her societie thou find'st
Attractive, human, rational, love still;
In loving thou dost well, in passion not,
Wherein true Love consists not; love refines
The thought, and heart enlarges, hath his seat
In Reason, and is judicious, is the scale
By which to heav'nly Love thou mayst ascend,
Not sunk in carnal pleasure, for which cause
Among the Beasts no Mate for thee was found.

[viii. 561-94

Waldock finds Raphael's sermon 'unpleasant' and 'dishonest'. Raphael, he complains, ignores most of what Adam
says and assumes there is no more in question than physical
attraction, and concludes by explaining 'wherein true Love
consists' as though Adam himself had not already done so.

Adam, 'half abasht' as Milton says, (Waldock sees no
reason why he should be, though it would seem natural in a
lover whose raptures have met with such a response)
defends himself:

Neither her out-side formd so fair, nor aught
In procreation common to all kindes
(Though higher of the genial Bed by far,
And with mysterious reverence I deem)
So much delights me as those graceful acts,
Those thousand decencies that daily flow
From all her words and actions, mixt with Love
And sweet compliance, which declare unfeignd
Union of Mind, or in us both one Soul.

[viii. 596-604

'May not one fairly suggest', asks Waldock, 'that a man
who speaks like this is passing Raphael's tests tolerably
well?' Certainly Adam here is expressing the poet's own
ideal of wedded love, and he is speaking sincerely. This is
the unfallen Adam and he is not yet guilty of the sensuality
Raphael has spoken of; but Raphael was diagnosing the

state of mind revealed in Adam's confession of the over-
powering effects of Eve's beauty, and warning him of its
danger. The danger he sees is Adam's Adoration of Eve,
and how if that adoration prevails so will sensuality. Adoration – idolatry: this is the sin Adam has confessed himself
liable to. And so Raphael's last word before he leaves him is
that the harmony of love will hold only while Adam loves
this side idolatry:

> Be strong, live happie, and love, but first of all
> Him whom to love is to obey.   [viii. 633–4

Waldock, favouring a different view – that of romantic,
chivalric love – complains that the poet does not consistently
represent this single, simple view. That seems to me an
unreasonable complaint. In the course of this dialogue we
are given a complex, complete and dramatic exposition of
human love in its various aspects; let us try to follow and
accept it so that we may enjoy the story as the poet tells it.

Chapter 10

THE FALL

With Raphael's departure Adam and Eve are left alone to face their trial. Their temptation and fall is a masterly narrative sequence, each incident proceeding naturally from the previous one. The doctrines that govern Milton's telling of the story are implicit throughout but it is the story itself that holds our attention.

It starts with Eve asserting her independence, and emerging as an individual character. She suggests to Adam, in all innocence, that they would get through more work if they worked apart:

> . . . what wonder if so near
> Looks intervene and smiles, or object new
> Casual discourse draw on . . .   [ix. 221–3

Adam demurs because of the danger of Eve's being found alone by the Enemy. Eve,

> As one who loves, and som unkindness meets,   [ix. 271

replies that Adam's reasons imply doubt of her 'firm faith' and 'love':

> Thoughts, which how found they harbour in thy brest
> *Adam*, misthought of her to thee so dear?   [ix. 288–9

Adam replies 'with healing words', pointing out that both are stronger when together:

> I from the influence of thy looks receive
> Access in every Vertue, . . .

Why shouldst not thou like sense within thee feel
When I am present . . . ?   [ix. 315–16

But Eve, still feeling herself undervalued,

Thus her reply with accent sweet renewd. [ix. 321

She is enjoying standing up to Adam in argument, and now
takes higher ground: what is the value of virtue that cannot
stand trial unaided?

And what is Faith, Love, Vertue unassayd
Alone, without exterior help sustaind?
Let us not then suspect our happie State
Left so imperfet by the Maker wise,
As not secure to single or combin'd:
Fraile is our happiness, if this be so,
And *Eden* were no *Eden* thus expos'd. [ix. 335–41

(Critics express surprise that the author should have forgotten what he wrote in *Areopagitica*: 'I cannot praise a
fugitive and cloister'd vertue, unexercis'd & unbreath'd,
that never sallies out and sees her adversary, but slinks out
of the race, where that immortall garland is to be run for,
not without dust and heat.' But they themselves forget that
there Milton was writing of fallen man and, equally important, that here it is Eve, not the narrator, who is speaking.) Adam replies 'fervently', trying to make her see things
in their true light:

O Woman, best are all things as the will
Of God ordaind them, his creating hand
Nothing imperfet or deficient left
Of all that he Created, much less Man,
Or aught that might his happie State secure,
Secure from outward force; within himself
The danger lies, yet lies within his power:
Against his will he can receive no harm.
                                    [ix. 343–50

The danger is of reason being deluded by 'som faire appear-
ing good':

> Not then mistrust, but tender love enjoins,
> That I should mind thee oft, and mind thou me.
>
> [ix. 357–8

'Mind' here means 'remind', that is of the danger. It is not
for us, Adam concludes, to seek temptation; 'trial will come
unsought'. If Eve would prove her constancy let her first
prove her obedience. Adam however has become a little
piqued by Eve's attitude (no doubt he sees she is still un-
willing to give way), and so he ends by saying that if she
still thinks that they will be less prepared for their trial if it
comes unexpectedly than if they go consciously to seek it,
then

> Go; for thy stay, not free, absents thee more.
>
> [ix. 372

Eve, cleverly ignoring the reluctance of Adam's consent,
accepts it with a submissive air:

> With thy permission then, and thus forewarnd . . .
> The willinger I go, nor much expect
> A Foe so proud will first the weaker seek;
> So bent, the more will shame him his repulse.
> Thus saying, from her Husbands hand her hand
> Soft she withdrew, . . .   [ix. 378–86

This scene has done all that is required of it. First Eve
has become an individual character, capable of acting on her
own. This is the Eve who will fall to the wiles of the Serpent
– confident, adventurous, argumentative, speculative, a
little irked at moments by her inferior position: these are
the proclivities Satan will play on so cunningly and surely.
Secondly the train of fatal events has been started without
calling in question the innocence of Adam or Eve. It is true
that Eve has opposed Adam and that he has yielded to her,

but these are not sins. Neither of them loses his temper, and
it is only after the Fall that they indulge in recriminations
about the incident; it is not until then that the poet admits
any word of blame (at the time he shows only pity), and
then it is they who, so humanly, blame each other.

Satan, lying in wait in the form of a serpent, is overjoyed
to catch sight of Eve alone,

> Veild in a Cloud of Fragrance, where she stood,
> Half spi'd, so thick the Roses bushing round
> About her glowd, . . .   [ix. 425–7

As she tends the flowers she is described as

>   mindless the while,
> Her self, though fairest unsupported Flowr,
> From her best prop so farr, and storm so nigh.
>   [ix. 431–3

Eve's mindlessness, her careless happiness, is one of her
charms, but it is also her most vulnerable point. She has
already forgotten her brush with Adam, and forgotten his
warning.

When the Serpent has succeeded in attracting her attention he addresses her in the extravagant language of
'courtly love'. Adam's adoration of Eve is now seen in
another light:

> Fairest resemblance of thy Maker fair,
> Thee all things living gaze on, all things thine
> By gift, and thy Celestial Beautie adore
> With ravishment beheld, . . .   [ix. 538–42

But there is only one man capable of discerning 'half what
in thee is fair':

>   who shouldst be seen
> A Goddess among Gods, ador'd and serv'd
> By Angels numberless, thy daily Train.
>   So gloz'd the Tempter, and his Proem tun'd;

Into the heart of *Eve* his words made way,
Though at the voice much marveling.   [ix. 546–51

In reply to her questions the Serpent tells how he has
attained to both speech and reason by eating of the fruit of
a certain tree; and then, resuming his strain of courtly love,
he tells her that, after considering all things in Earth and
Heaven with 'capacious mind', he found nothing so good
and fair as she, and was compelled to come and worship her.
With pleased feminine dignity Eve puts aside the adulation,
but she is now urged by curiosity to behold the miraculous
tree:

But say, where grows the Tree, from hence how far? . . .
To whom the wilie Adder, blithe and glad.
Empress, the way is readie, and not long . . .
Lead then, said *Eve*.   [ix. 617–31

When they come to the tree and Eve sees what tree it is,
she, 'yet sinless' as the poet says, briefly tells the Serpent of
the prohibition, in a matter-of-fact manner indicating that
this is an end of the matter. But whilst she is guilelessly
instructing him, he is all impatience to start casting his
spells to confound her:

and as to passion mov'd
Fluctuats disturbd, yet comely, and in act
Rais'd, as of som great matter to begin.
As when of old som Orator renownd
In *Athens* or free *Rome* . . .
. . . to som great cause addrest,
Stood in himself collected, while each part,
Motion, each act won audience ere the tongue,
Somtimes in highth began, as no delay
Of Preface brooking through his Zeal of Right.
    [ix. 667–76

Here as usual Milton uses a simile as a transposed description of what would otherwise be unimaginable; this image

remains in the mind, and it is as an orator rather than as a snake that we see Satan during the speeches that follow and throughout the scene of the temptation.

Satan's opening speech is a brilliant feat of sophistry, proceeding from the lie, which Eve has no means of detecting, that he himself has tasted the fruit. His aim is to tempt her with the ambition to improve her lot, as he has improved his, through forbidden knowledge. In order to succeed he must remove her fear of disobeying God's command; and this entails making her sceptical of the reality of death and evil and, above all, of a supreme and righteous Ruler. His arguments play bewilderingly in and out of each other.

He starts by assuring her, 'Ye shall not die':

> look on mee,
> Mee who have toucht and tasted, yet both live
> And life more perfet have attaind . . .   [ix. 687–9

Will God be angry at your doing likewise? Will he not rather praise your courage in risking death ('whatever thing Death be') in order to achieve a higher and happier life by knowledge of good and evil?

> Of good, how just? of evil, if what is evil
> Be real, why not known, since easier shunnd?
> God therefore cannot hurt ye, and be just;
> Not just, not God; not fear'd then, nor obey'd . . .
> Why then was this forbid? Why but to awe,
> Why but to keep ye low and ignorant,
> His worshippers; he knows that in the day
> Ye Eate thereof, your Eyes that seem so clear,
> Yet are but dim, shall perfetly be then
> Opend and clear'd, and ye shall be as Gods,
> Knowing both Good and Evil as they know.
>   [ix. 698–709

Perhaps that is all death means, putting off humanity for divinity. And what are the gods anyway, that man should not become as they? Because they existed before you they pretend to have created you and your world: 'I question it', says Satan, for I see this world producing everything of itself, they nothing. The way Satan shifts back and forth between one God and gods illustrates his technique of confusing the issues.

Eve is left gazing fascinated at the fruit, convinced by the Tempter's arguments and with appetite now prompting her to eat; appetite, it has often been pointed out, only comes in as an incentive after her mind has succumbed; the temptation has been entirely mental. It is nevertheless significant that appetite, sensual desire, should assail her just at this point, when reason has surrendered. Before she plucks the fruit she does indeed pause to reason with herself, but only to justify what she is intent on doing. Her reasoning shows her mind entirely dominated by Satan's; her arguments merely echo his. Her train of thought leads her on not only to deny God but to accept the Serpent as her benefactor: he, unlike God,

> envies not, but brings with joy
> The good befall'n him, . . .   [ix. 770–1]

She has turned Satanist.

As Eve plucks and eats the fruit Satan is seen again as a snake and contemptuously dismissed from the scene:

> Back to the Thicket slunk
> The guiltie Serpent, and well might, for *Eve*
> Intent now wholly on her taste, naught else
> Regarded, such delight till then, as seemd,
> In Fruit she never tasted, whether true
> Or fancied so, through expectation high
> Of knowledge, nor was God-head from her thought.
> Greedily she ingorg'd without restraint,
> And knew not eating Death.   [ix. 784–92

Here is the immediate delight in sinning, its 'sweet fruition',

[172]

the reckless flood of joy and the hubris, which the poet expresses in terms of intoxication:

> hightend as with Wine, jocond and boon.   [ix. 793

Even after the Fall Eve remains an attractive figure. But the poet nevertheless has to show how her mind and nature, and her relationship to Adam, have been altered by sin. After paying her devotions to the Tree and mocking at God in a manner Satan has taught her, Adam comes into her thoughts for the first time since she left him: shall she share her good fortune with him or 'keep the odds of knowledge in my power'?

>   so to add what wants
> In Femal Sex, the more to draw his Love,
> And render me more equal, and perhaps,
> A thing not undesireable, somtime
> Superior; for inferior who is free?
> This may be well: but what if God have seen
> And Death ensue? then I shall be no more,
> And *Adam* wedded to another *Eve*
> Shall live with her enjoying, I extinct;
> A death to think. Confirmd then I resolve,
> *Adam* shall share with me in bliss or woe:
> So dear I love him, that with him all deaths
> I could endure, without him live no life.   [ix. 821–33

'So dear I love him' is genuine; and we must remember that her love not only brings about Adam's fall but in the end brings about their reconciliation to each other and to God. Nevertheless all her thoughts at the moment are self-regarding; it is what *she* will gain or lose that occupies her. This selfishness in love is a direct and unavoidable effect of the situation created by her fall; her love can now act in only one of two ways, by giving up Adam or by betraying him. Adam will be faced with a similar dilemma. The human

[173]

situation has been corrupted: that is the fact to remember as we come to Adam's ordeal.

Not far from the Tree Eve sees Adam coming in search of her and runs to meet him. What she says is a mixture of love and wiliness, giving a spirited portrait of a woman in action:

> Hast thou not wonderd, *Adam*, at my stay?
> Thee I have misst, and thought it long, depriv'd
> Thy presence, agonie of love till now
> Not felt, . . .   [ix. 856–9

This, coldly considered, is a lie; until a few moments ago she had not thought of him at all. But the deceit is perhaps only half conscious; it is what she feels at the moment, and as always with Eve it is her feeling that counts. Her thinking may be confused and tricky but her feelings are always clear and direct. She then tells what she has done and of the marvellous effects of the fruit, adding what this time I'm afraid is an outright lie, 'which for thee Chiefly I sought'.

Adam stands stupified:

> From his slack hand the Garland wreath'd for *Eve*
> Down dropd, and all the faded Roses shed:
> Speechless he stood, and pale, till thus at length
> First to himself he inward silence broke.   [ix. 892–5

Having bewailed the fact that Eve is lost, he instantly accepts the consequence that he is lost with her; there is no hesitation, no struggle:

>   som cursed fraud
> Of Enemie hath beguil'd thee, yet unknown,
> And mee with thee hath ruind, for with thee
> Certain my resolution is to Die;
> How can I live without thee, how forgoe
> Thy sweet Converse and Love so dearly joind,
> To live again in these wilde Woods forlorn?
> Should God create another *Eve*, and I

Another Rib afford, yet love of thee
Would never from my heart; no, no, I feel
The Link of Nature draw me: Flesh of Flesh,
Bone of my Bone thou art, and from thy State
Mine never shall be parted, bliss or woe. [ix. 904–16

'If Adam's words', comments Waldock, 'are allowed to have the meanings that words usually have in English, these lines mean love.' Of course they do, and that is what makes the tension of this tragic situation. Confronted by this awful dilemma Adam takes what seems, under the stress of his feeling, the only possible decision. The poet himself speaks of his hero

Submitting to what seemd remediless. [ix. 919

His decision taken, Adam recovers from the stupor of shock and can think again:

Bold deed thou hast presum'd, adventrous *Eve*,
And peril great provok't, . . .
But past who can recall, or don undoe?
Not God Omnipotent, nor Fate, . . . [ix. 921–7

This is the cold truth, but he tries to reassure Eve and himself by arguing away the consequences of her deed. Perhaps she will not die; perhaps her offence was not so heinous since the fruit had already been profaned by the Serpent; in any case the Serpent has not died but attained to higher life, and so perhaps may they.

Nor can I think that God, Creator wise,
Though threatning, will in earnest so destroye
Us his prime Creatures, . . .
. . . lest the Adversary
Triumph and say; Fickle their State whom God
Most favours, who can please him long? [ix. 937–49

These desperate reasonings show where Adam's resolve has placed him, for they are the same Satan had used to tempt

Eve, and he ends on a note of Satanic mockery of God. He is, however, far from convinced by this attempt to talk himself out of the situation: he is 'not deceiv'd'. This is apparent from his abruptly dismissing all such speculations as irrelevant to his purpose:

> However I with thee have fixt my Lot,
> Certain to undergo like doom; if Death
> Consort with thee, Death is to mee as Life;
> So forcible within my heart I feel
> The Bond of Nature draw me to my own,
> My own in thee, for what thou art is mine;
> Our State cannot be severd, we are one,
> One Flesh; to lose thee were to lose my self.
>   [ix. 952-9

These words are as irresistible as those of his silent resolution not to desert Eve, and leave us in no doubt of the compulsion of his love; and it is love untouched by sensuality. The poet is putting the issue in its most extreme form, piling up the odds as he moves to the climax of his story.

Eve, who has been silent all this time but certainly not out of the picture, now breaks out in praise of Adam's 'exceeding love':

> So saying she embrac'd him, and for joye
> Tenderly wept, much won that he his Love
> Had so enobl'd, as of choice to incurr
> Divine displeasure for her sake, or Death . . .
> She gave him of that fair enticing Fruit
> With liberal hand: he scrupl'd not to eat
> Against his better knowledge, not deceiv'd,
> But fondly overcome with Femal charm.   [ix. 990-9

Waldock quotes with approval Tillyard's remark (since retracted) that 'the last line is curiously inconsistent with what went before'. It is, says Waldock, 'oddly out of harmony with what we have just been reading, especially with the two key passages that have revealed to us the motions of Adam's heart. . . . "Fondly overcome with Femal charm" is simply Milton's comment on the recent course of events: events the true nature of which he has just been demonstrating to us. . . . Adam's words ring so true that they *prove* to us his feelings, and against proof of that kind no comment can – or ought – to prevail. . . . Adam falls through love . . . , through love as human beings know it at its best, through true love, through the kind of love that Raphael has told Adam,

> is the scale
> By which to heav'nly Love thou maist ascend.'

First let us make sure that we know what the offending words mean. 'Against his better knowledge, not deceiv'd', that is as Eve was by Satan; Adam knows what he is doing, sins with his eyes open. 'Femal charm' is the seemingly preternatural, the irresistible power Eve exercises over him; and as he had told Raphael, this is a matter not only of her physical attractions but of all she means to him as the companion of his life – all that is expressed again in those two passages of passionate refusal to desert her. From the humanistic standpoint this may be 'love as human beings know it at its best'; but it is not for Milton the kind of love that leads up to heavenly love, any more than the love of Paolo and Francesca is for Dante. Adam prefers his love of Eve to love of God, and the immediate consequence is the corruption of the love he prizes so highly. As he eats the fruit he, like Eve before him, is all sensual appetite, and the immediate sequel is lust – 'in Lust they burne'. This is what Raphael had warned him of.

To say then that 'fondly overcome with Femal charm' is inconsistent with what went before is to say the reverse of the truth. As to Waldock's distinction between demonstration and comment, comment in narrative poetry is a proper

[177]

means of demonstration if it comes at the right moment, with the whole force of the argument and its action behind it. Here the comment falls like a hammer hitting its nail home; it is the consummation of the argument that started in Book VIII and has been worked out in the story. Milton has not once swerved from his course, even while living and pleading as Adam: he has kept control and brought us to his own foreseen conclusion. Of course Adam's words 'prove to us his feelings'; but Waldock assumes that they prove more, that they prove Adam to be in the right. This is a pathetic fallacy the great poet does not fall into; he feels strongly, thinks strongly and sees truly. Waldock on the contrary supposes that his irrepressible humanity unconsciously betrayed Milton into a sympathy with Adam that founders his conscious intentions. I find it more sensible to assume that so deliberate an artist as Milton knew just what he was about. Supposing he had not let Adam speak in a way that warms our hearts and commands our sympathy, making us feel that he has no alternative but to act as he does, where then would have been the force of the situation, where the moral? We must feel to the full Adam's predicament, feel that he has no choice, before the poet comes down with his stern and measured judgement. We do not like it; it hurts our susceptibilities; it shocks us as, in a contrary way (not acting 'against his better knowledge') Aeneas's desertion of Dido shocks us. Like Virgil, Milton puts religious duty above human desires.

Chapter 11

AFTER THE FALL

In the remainder of Book IX and Book X the nature and meaning of the Fall is portrayed through the effects on Adam and Eve and on their relationship. These effects constitute spiritual as distinct from bodily death, which Milton explains in Chapter XII of *The Christian Doctrine*: 'The second degree of death is called spiritual death; by which is meant the loss of divine grace, and that of innate righteousness, wherein man in the beginning lived unto God. . . . And this death took place not only on the very day, but at the very moment of the fall. . . . This death consists, first, in the loss, or at least in the obscuration to a great extent of that right reason which enabled man to discern the chief good, and in which consisted as it were the life of the understanding. . . . It consists, secondly, in that deprivation of righteousness and liberty to do good, and in that slavish subjection to sin and the devil, which constitutes, as it were, the death of the will. . . . Lastly, sin is its own punishment, and produces, in its natural consequences, the death of the spiritual life; and more especially gross and habitual sin.'

The first effect of eating the fruit is that Adam and Eve are overcome by sexual desire:

> hee on *Eve*
> Began to cast lascivious Eyes, she him
> As wantonly repaid; in Lust they burne:
> Till *Adam* thus gan *Eve* to dalliance move.
>
> [ix. 1013–16

[179]

Adam assumes the role of witty gallant, making fun of holy
things; and Eve has become for him a woman to 'enjoy'.
Carnal desire is now valued and pursued for its own sake:

> if such pleasure be
> In things to us forbidden, it might be wisht
> For this one Tree had bin forbidden ten.
> But come, so well refresht, now let us play,
> As meet is, after such delicious Fare;
> For never did thy Beautie since the day
> I saw thee first and wedded thee, adornd
> With all perfections, so enflame my sense
> With ardor to enjoy thee.   [ix. 1024–32

With the words 'Her hand he seiz'd' we recall the description of them as first seen in Paradise:

> Thus talking hand in hand alone they passd
> On to thir blissful Bower.   [iv. 689–90

Having indulged their lust they wake to the consciousness
of lost innocence. With innocence gone the dignity and
confidence of innate goodness has been replaced by the
confusion and weakness of shame:

> and each the other viewing
> Soon found thir Eyes how opend, and thir minds
> How darkend; innocence, that as a veil
> Had shaddowd them from knowing ill, was gon,
> . . . They destitute and bare
> Of all thir vertue, silent, and in face
> Confounded long they sate, as strucken mute, . . .
>   [ix. 1052–64

The degradation of guilty shame is summed up in the
estrangement from God and Heaven, and in the desire to
hide like a wounded animal. Adam says,

> How shall I behold the face
> Henceforth of God or Angel, erst with joy

[180]

And rapture so oft beheld? those heav'nly shapes
Will dazle now this earthly, with thir blaze
Insufferably bright. O might I here
In solitude live savage, in som glade
Obscur'd, where highest Woods impenetrable
To Starr or Sun-light, spread thir umbrage broad
And brown as Ev'ning: Cover me ye Pines,
Ye Cedars, with innumerable boughes
Hide me, where I may never see them more.
[ix. 1080–90

They cover their nakedness —

O how unlike
To that first naked Glorie –   [ix. 1114–15

but the mental effects of guilty shame are not thereby eased.
The mind of man no longer moves in obedience to right
reason; the passions have seized control and thrown his
whole state into anarchy. They are no longer natural
masters of themselves:

They sate them down to weep, nor onely Teares
Raind at thir Eyes, but high Winds worse within
Began to rise, high Passions, Anger, Hate,
Mistrust, Suspicion, Discord, and shook sore
Thir inward State of Mind, calm Region once
And full of Peace, now tost and turbulent.
[ix. 1120–6

They fall to quarrelling, and blame each other for what has
happened. Adam first reproaches Eve:

Would thou hadst hearkend to my words, and stayd
With me, as I besought thee, when that strange
Desire of wandring this unhappie Morn,
I know not whence possessd thee.   [ix. 1134–7

To which Eve, 'soon mov'd with touch of blame', retorts
that it

> might as ill have happend thou being by,
> Or to thy self perhaps.   [ix. 1147–8

In any case

> Was I to have never parted from thy side?
> As good have grown there still a liveless Rib.
>   [ix. 1153–4

Then with feminine nimbleness she shifts ground for the home-thrust:

> Being as I am, why didst not thou the Head
> Command me absolutely not to go,
> Going into such danger as thou saidst?
> Too facil then thou didst not much gainsay,
> Nay didst permit, approve, and fair dismiss.
>   [ix. 1155–9

The unkindest cut of all is 'facil', which in *Paradise Regain'd* Milton applies to Eve herself.

> To whom then first incenst *Adam* repli'd.
> Is this the Love, is this the recompense
> Of mine to thee, ingrateful Eve, exprest
> Immutable when thou wert lost, not I . . . ?
>   [ix. 1163–5

Their 'sweet Converse and Love so dearly joind' has turned to hatred and recrimination.

In Book X the description of Adam and Eve as they appear before the Son for judgment sums up what has been enacted in the latter part of Book IX:

> Love was not in thir looks, either to God
> Or to each other, but apparent guilt
> And shame and perturbation and despair,
> Anger and obstinacie and hate and guile. [x. 111–14

They are sentenced to sorrow and labour and death. Eve is an affecting sight as she is questioned by her Lord:

> To whom sad *Eve* with shame nigh overwhelmd,
> Confessing soon, yet not before her Judge
> Bold or loquacious, thus abasht repli'd.
>   The Serpent me beguil'd and I did eat.
>   [x. 159–62

The sentence passed on the Serpent contains the prophecy that the seed of the woman shall bruise his head, the meaning of which is only gradually revealed to them by Michael in the course of the last two Books.

Sin and Death now invade the world in person, and all nature is afflicted with a curse on account of man's sin. Adam is aware of the 'growing miseries' in the world about him – inclemencies of weather, the warring of beast with beast, and the hostility of beast to man:

>   nor stood much in awe
> Of Man, but fled him, or with count'nance grim
> Glar'd on him passing.   [x. 712–14

Adam however is only vaguely conscious of these surrounding events; he is preoccupied with his inward misery.

He now realizes to the full his fallen condition and its consequences, and in a long tormented soliloquy he wrestles with his guilty despair; we see the agonies of a soul desperately trying to find a way out of the pit. He questions the justice of a God who can overwhelm his creature with endless punishment. Not only must he himself face a life of utter misery but all his progeny must endure the like, and curse him for it, to the end of time:

> All that I eat or drink or shall beget
> Is propagated curse.   x. 728–9

He cries out to be relieved of this cruel burden of life, for which he never asked:

> Why am I mockt with death, and lengthened out
> To deathless pain? how gladly would I meet

[183]

Mortalitie my sentence, and be Earth
Insensible.   [x. 774–7

This prompts him to speculate on what death is. He realizes
that death may be spiritual as well as physical, and that he
is already suffering spiritual death:

But say
That Death be not one stroke, as I suppos'd,
Bereaving sense, but endless miserie
From this day onward, which I feel begun
Both in me and without me, and so last
To perpetuitie.   [x. 808–13

But why, he asks again – this is the most tormenting point,
to which he recurs – should guiltless posterity be condemned for his fault? But he sees that the answer is that no
offspring of his can be guiltless:

But from me what can proceed,
But all corrupt, both Mind and Will deprav'd,
Not to doe only, but to will the same
With me? . . . first and last
On mee, mee onely, as the source and spring
Of all corruption, all the blame lights due;
So might the wrauth. Fond wish! couldst thou support
That burden heavier than the Earth to bear,
Than all the World much heavier, though divided
With that bad Woman?   [x. 824–37

He can see no end to the woes he has brought on himself and
all mankind, no way out, yet he submits to God's will and
vindicates his justice. He has made his own way to a
position from which he will understand at once and to the
full the joyful tidings eventually revealed to him by Michael
of how the world is to be saved. This is the first stage in
his moral recovery: he has faced the situation and accepted
his responsibility, though he realizes that he himself can do
nothing to relieve fallen man's estate. Adam's moral and

[184]

intellectual stature shows here more convincingly than ever it could do before the Fall.

If we compare his soliloquy with Satan's at the beginning of Book IV, when 'conscience wakes despair', Adam's submission may to some appear less heroic than Satan's defiance of his doom; but for Milton it is not less but more heroic, 'the better fortitude of patience'. Adam is still self-centred, preoccupied with his own misery, but the way is now open to repentance and a return to God. This next stage in his recovery is effected by Eve.

Eve approaches Adam to console him, and all his passion of guilty despair vents itself in hatred and loathing of her:

> Out of my sight, thou Serpent !   [x. 867

'Serpent' is a cruel thrust, as shrewd as Eve's 'facil'. The egotism of his misery is clearly seen:

> But for thee
> I had persisted happie, . . .   [x. 873–4

He vituperates her, and goes on to deliver a prophetic diatribe on all that men will suffer at the hands of women,

> linkt and Wedlock-bound
> To a fell Adversarie, his hate or shame.
>   [x. 905–6

Critics of course say that this is just Milton voicing his own views on women. But Adam's outburst should be read dramatically, and is then seen to be right. Those who wish to deduce from the poem Milton's view of women should take into account what follows. If it was Eve who betrayed their love it is now Eve who retrieves and saves it. On this point it is best to cite a woman. Helen Darbishire in 'Milton's *Paradise Lost*' (1951), has said that Eve's love for Adam 'has taught her true humility and repentance. Its passionate unselfishness lifts her above Adam. When he besought God to let him bear the whole burden he included

[185]

with himself "that bad woman". When she beseeches it is
Adam she yearns to spare.' I will quote the whole passage,
one of the most crucial in the poem:

> He added not, and from her turnd, but *Eve*
> Not so repulst, with Tears that ceas'd not flowing,
> And tresses all disorderd, at his feet
> Fell humble, and imbracing them, besought
> His peace, and thus proceeded in her plaint.
>   Forsake me not thus, *Adam*, witness Heav'n
> What love sincere and reverence in my heart
> I bear thee, and unweeting have offended,
> Unhappilie deceiv'd; thy suppliant
> I beg, and clasp thy knees; bereave me not,
> Whereon I live, thy gentle looks, thy aid,
> Thy counsel in this uttermost distress,
> My onely strength and stay: forlorn of thee,
> Whither shall I betake me, where subsist?
> While yet we live, scarce one short hour perhaps,
> Between us two let there be peace, both joining,
> As joind in injuries, one enmitie
> Against a Foe by doom express assign'd us,
> That cruel Serpent: On mee exercise not
> Thy hatred for this miserie befall'n,
> On me already lost, mee than thy self
> More miserable; both have sinnd, but thou
> Against God onely, I against God and thee,
> And to the place of judgement will return,
> There with my cries importune Heaven, that all
> The sentence from thy head remov'd may light
> On me, sole cause to thee of all this woe,
> Mee mee onely just object of his ire.   [x. 909–36

Landor says of the last line. . . . 'At last her voice fails her,
. . . Similar, in the trepidation of grief, is Virgil's "Me, me,
adsum qui feci".'

> She ended weeping, and her lowlie plight,
> Immoveable till peace obtain from fault

Acknowledg'd and deplor'd, in *Adam* wrought
Commiseration; soon his heart relented
Towards her, his life so late and sole delight,
Now at his feet submissive in distress,
Creature so faire his reconcilement seeking,
His counsel whom she had displeas'd, his aid;
As one disarmd, his anger all he lost,
And thus with peaceful words uprais'd her soon.
[x. 937–46

'In their utmost despair', comments Helen Darbishire, 'it is
Eve who by her love is the means not only of reconciling
Adam to herself but of reconciling them both to God. Let
this be remembered by those who accuse Milton of contempt for women.' This is well said, and I differ only on one
point. To say that Eve's love reconciles them both to God is
too summary a statement to be quite accurate, though it is
only so in omitting the last step, which is permissible in a
lecture into which so much has to be packed and is. Eve's
love makes their reconciliation to God possible by removing
the hardness and bitterness from Adam's heart, by reviving
the human love that can alone reopen the way to the love of
God; but it is at this point that Adam again takes command,
reasserting the intellectual and moral superiority which Eve
herself recognizes. One notes in Eve's speech the echo of
that offending line:

Hee for God onely, shee for God in him.

We must accept with Eve the fact of Adam's superiority
unless we are to think the humility of her love is a false
humility. Adam's superiority at this point is due to his
having faced and recognized and submitted to the new
conditions of life, and it is he therefore who now instructs
Eve to submit and turn to God. Eve at the moment is intent
on finding ways of avoiding the consequences of their sin,
though she is thinking of others and willing to sacrifice

herself. First she wishes to save Adam from those consequences by drawing all the punishment on herself; but he
has previously realized the presumptuousness of a similar
desire in himself. He reproves her 'fond wish' but immediately softens the reproof with words of loving-kindness more
poignant than his raptures of love before the Fall:

> But rise, let us no more contend, nor blame
> Each other, blam'd anough elsewhere, but strive
> In offices of Love, how we may light'n
> Each others burden in our share of woe.   [x. 958–61

Adam's reawakened love has already adapted itself to the
new conditions of life. Eve however goes on to suggest that
they could prevent the future miseries of mankind by remaining childless, or by suicide:

> But if thou judge it hard and difficult,
> Conversing, looking, loving, to abstain
> From Loves due Rites, nuptial imbraces sweet,
> And with desire to languish without hope,
> . . . let us make short,
> Let us seek Death, . . .   [x. 992–1001

Adam has been through all this, and knows that it is useless
to kick against the pricks, that they cannot out-wit their
fate; and he points out to Eve that her seeming contempt
of life and pleasure reveals

> Not thy contempt, but anguish and regret
> From loss of life and pleasure overlov'd . . .
> No more be mentiond then of violence
> Against our selves, and wilful barrenness,
> That cuts us off from hope, and savours onely
> Rancor and pride, impatience and despite,
> Reluctance against God and his just yoke
> Laid on our Necks. Remember with what mild
> And gracious temper he both heard and judg'd
> Without wrauth or reviling.   [x. 1018–48

Let them throw themselves then on God's mercy, ask his
help to face life in their fallen condition, and pray for his
forgiveness:

> What better can we do, than to the place
> Repairing where he judg'd us, prostrate fall
> Before him reverent, and there confess
> Humbly our faults, and pardon beg, with teares
> Watering the ground, and with our sighs the Air
> Frequenting, sent from hearts contrite, in sign
> Of sorrow unfeignd, and humiliation meek.   [x. 1086–92

The repetition of these lines to describe the act itself brings
the Book and the story of the Fall to a full close:

> . . . they forthwith to the place
> Repairing where he judg'd them, prostrate fell
> Before him reverent, and both confessd
> Humbly thir faults, and pardon beggd, with teares
> Watering the ground, and with thir sighs the Air
> Frequenting, sent from hearts contrite, in sign
> Of sorrow unfeignd, and humiliation meek.
>   [x. 1098–1104

Chapter 12

THE LAST TWO BOOKS

The last two Books of the poem have always been felt to be flat and disappointing. Addison, though he does not agree, mentions it as a common opinion in his day: 'I have been the more particular in my Quotations out of the Eleventh Book of *Paradise Lost,* because it is not generally reckoned among the most shining Books of the Poem. For which reason, the Reader might be apt to overlook those many Passages in it, which deserve our Admiration ... these last two Books can by no means be looked upon as unequal Parts of this divine Poem' (*Spectator,* No. 363). He admits that the change from vision in Book XI to narration in Book XII as a method of presenting the future history of mankind 'is as if an History Painter should put in Colours one half of his Subject, and write down the remaining part of it. If *Milton's* Poem flags anywhere, it is in this Narration, where in some places the Author has been so attentive to his Divinity, that he has neglected his Poetry. The Narration, however, rises very happily on several Occasions' (*Spectator,* No. 369).

It is generally agreed that the matter of these Books – the revelation to Adam of God's plan for man's salvation down to the Redemption and to the Second Coming of Christ – is essential to the argument of the poem; but until recently there has never been a plausible explanation of what is felt to be their artistic failure. The usual explanation is that there has been a flagging of imagination and a failure of style, which in the case of a major poet is not an explanation but an improbable hypothesis. Thus C. S. Lewis is

[190]

reduced to saying 'we must be content to say that Milton's talent temporarily failed him, just as Wordsworth's talent failed in later life. . . . Perhaps Milton was in ill health. Perhaps, being old, he yielded to a natural, though disastrous, impatience to get the work finished.' The analogy with Wordsworth is off beam; and the words smack too much of Mark Pattison's explanation of what he thought the failure of *Samson Agonistes*. There is in fact, as Addison saw, no failure of style in these last Books; Milton still commands his epic style in all its variety of mood and manner. Yet there is a cause for the effect of these Books on the common reader that stares one in the face: it is, that though the matter is essential to the argument it has not been brought within the action, and could not be. So far the action has been a unity narrowing down from the revolt of the angels and the scenes in Heaven to the creation of the world, and so to the human drama of Adam and Eve; we have grown familiar with the few scenes and characters, have become sure of the course and bounds of the story. And now suddenly, at the last moment, just when we might expect the final fall of the curtain, we are switched away to a panorama of scenes and events in which the previous actors do not figure at all, of which even Adam is only a spectator. How can we at this late point in the story become interested in a procession of characters and events outside the framework of the story – Cain and Abel, Enoch, Noah and the Flood, the Tower of Babel, Abraham, Moses and David, and all their doings? When this long interlude is over the poem is concluded in some fifty lines, and all readers find that with this return to the story proper the poetic interest revives in a tell-tale manner.

It will be sufficient just to mention one plea made for this episode. Addison pointed out, and others have followed him, that there was a precedent for Milton's vision of futurity in the *Sixth Aeneid*, when Anchises presents to Aeneas in

Hades the shades of those heroes who are to descend from him, and prophecies the future greatness and glory of Rome. This is indeed a precedent for Milton's intent but hardly for his design. Virgil's is a short episode of some fifty lines in the very middle of the poem; Milton's episode occupies some 1,150 lines just before the close.

F. T. Prince is the first critic to have justified these Books as an integral and effective part of the poem as a whole (*Essays and Studies*, 1958). His essay is one of those definitive pieces of criticism which stands like a lion in the way of anyone else trying to handle the subject, and I shall avail myself of it to an improper extent in this last chapter. First, he answers my objection that this pageant of the future history of the world is outside the action, by observing that Milton here follows his usual method of dramatization: 'Everything in *Paradise Lost* is presented dramatically, that is, as it affects one or other of the characters (the method is not very different from that of Henry James). In Milton's purpose of renewing our vision, the characters of Adam and Eve have been particularly useful as "registers" of consciousness; so we have Adam's description of his first impressions of Paradise and of his feelings for Eve, and Eve's corresponding account of her first sensations, her first sight of Adam, and her love for him. . . . Looked at in this way, Books XI and XII are certainly a part of Adam's story, of the evolution of his consciousness. To paraphrase T. S. Eliot's remark on his own Tiresias, "What Adam *sees*, in fact is the substance of the poem". The selection of what he is to see from the reaches of future history is thus determined: he must be given an outline of the spiritual history of mankind, with the emphasis on those points which will give him the right attitude of hope, patience and effort.'

This view may not, does not I think, remove the awkwardness in the placing of this long interlude or of our having to attend so belatedly to this crowded pageant of people and events outside the straight story; but there was no other way of doing it – at any rate no one has ever suggested one – and the reader who adapts himself to the point of view indicated by Prince will appreciate the merits of these last Books and their contribution to the design and total effect of the poem. He will see that this outline of the Old and New Testaments, presenting the scheme of Christian salvation, is necessary to the completion not only of the argument but of the story, of the fate of Adam and Eve; which answers the gist of what was felt to be wrong with these Books. The only question that then remains is whether they do what is required of them as well as it could be done. We shall find that, though there are places in the earlier part of Book XII where the narrative drags, chiefly because the story of the Israelites is not as exciting to the modern reader as to Milton and his times, yet in the main there is no falling off in the poetic interest.

Book XI opens with Adam and Eve still in the posture of penitence in which they were left at the conclusion of Book X, but their sighs have been transformed by God's grace to prayers. The Son speaks to the Father of these mute prayers sent from contrite hearts as more pleasing than all the fruits of Paradise 'ere fall'n from innocence' – a more authoritative expression of the *felix culpa* doctrine than Adam's later outburst; and he speaks of the time when

> with mee
> All my redeemd may dwell in joy and bliss,
> Made one with me as I with thee am one.
>
> [xi. 42–4

Here is the purpose of these last Books, to reveal to Adam and Eve God's plan for man's redemption by the sacrifice of his only Son, and so to send them forth into the lower world fortified with hope and faith to endure their lot. Michael is sent to expel Adam and Eve from Eden, but

[193]

only after revealing to them the history of the world to the end of time:

> So send them forth, though sorrowing, yet in peace.
> [xi. 117

The scene between Adam and Eve before Michael's arrival is an effective introduction to all that follows, and shows their need for instruction; it is a scene of pathos. With the dawn of a new day they rise from their prayers with fresh hope and joy, conscious once more of God's favour. They feel again the beauty and peace and security of Paradise, just when they are about to be expelled from it. Adam glories and rejoices again in Eve; Eve is eager for them to recommence their customary work in the Garden,

> Though after sleepless night; for see the Morn
> All unconcerned with our unrest, begins
> Her rosie progress smiling; let us forth,
> I never from thy side henceforth to stray, . . .
> [xi. 173–6

But the air suddenly darkens,

>   Aire suddenly eclips'd
> After short blush of Morn,   [xi. 183–4

and they see an eagle and a lion each pursuing its prey towards the eastern Gate of Paradise, from which they themselves are soon to depart. As the sun is obscured in the east the western sky is lit by the bright chariot cloud of Michael and his descending angels. Adam reads these omens aright, as portending a further change in their condition:

> Us haply too secure of our discharge
> From penaltie.   [xi. 196–7

When Michael tells them that he has come to remove them from Paradise Adam is stunned and speechless, as when he met Eve returning with the forbidden fruit; but Eve characteristically breaks out in 'audible lament':

[194]

O unexpected stroke, worse than of Death!
Must I thus leave thee Paradise? thus leave
Thee Native Soil, these happie Walks and Shades,
Fit haunt of Gods? where I had hope to spend,
Quiet though sad, the respit of that day
That must be mortal to us both. O flowrs,
That never will in other Climat grow,
My early visitation, and my last
At Ev'n, which I bred up with tender hand
From the first op'ning bud, and gave ye Names,
Who now shall reare ye to the Sun, or rank
Your Tribes, and water from th' ambrosial Fount?
Thee lastly nuptial Bowr, by mee adornd
With what to sight or smell was sweet; from thee
How shall I part, and whither wander down
Into a lower World, to this obscure
And wild, how shall we breathe in other Aire
Less pure, accustomd to immortal Fruits?

[xi. 268–85

Adam accepts their banishment submissively. His great
regret is the banishment from God's presence; but Michael
assures him that God is everywhere, even in the lower world.
He tells him that he has been sent

To shew thee what shall come in future days
To thee and to thy Offspring; good with bad
Expect to hear, supernal Grace contending
With sinfulness of Men; thereby to learn
True patience, and to temper joy with fear
And pious sorrow, . . .   [xi. 357–62

Leaving Eve asleep, Michael leads Adam to the Hill of
Visions, from whose top they survey the 'Hemisphere of
Earth'. The similar panorama of the kingdoms of the world
shown to Jesus by Satan in *Paradise Regain'd* helps once
again to define the theme of these last two Books of *Paradise
Lost*:

His Eye might there command wherever stood
City of old or modern Fame, the Seat
Of mightiest Empire, from the destind Walls
Of *Cambalu*, seat of *Cathaian Can*
And *Samarchand* by *Oxus, Temirs* Throne,
To *Paquin* of *Sinaean* Kings, and thence
To *Agra* and *Lahor* of great *Mogul*
Down to the golden *Chersonese*, or where
The *Persian* in *Ecbatan* sate, or since
In *Hispahan*, or where the *Russian Ksar*
In *Mosco*, or the Sultan in *Bizance*,
Turchestan-born; nor could his eye not ken
Th' Empire of *Negus* to his utmost Port
Ercoco and the less Maritim Kings
Mombaza, and *Quiloa*, and *Melind*,
And *Sofala* thought *Ophir*, to the Realm
Of *Congo*, and *Angola* fardest South;
Or thence from *Niger* Flood to *Atlas* Mount
The Kingdoms of *Almansor*, *Fez* and *Sus*,
Marocco and *Algiers*, and *Tremisen*;
On Europe thence, and where *Rome* was to sway
The World.   [xi. 385–406

T. S. Eliot's own vision failed him when he said he could
enjoy the roll call of these names 'but I feel this is not serious
poetry, not poetry fully occupied about its business, but
rather a solemn game'. It is time we stopped talking about
Milton's delight in a string of sonorous proper names, as
though this was all it amounted to, and attended to the
import of such masterly shows of time and space. This
present magnificent geographical survey of the ancient
world, enlivened with the names of famous cities and peoples
and kingdoms – from the Arctic south through central Asia
and China, to India and the Moluccas, to Asia Minor;
round Africa to the Mediterranean, with finally the history
of Europe summed up in the one name of Rome – this
prelude, as Prince says, 'sets the scene for a series of far-

sweeping visions, of men and nations moving across mountains and plains, of civilizations rising and flourishing,
fighting and falling. Here it contributes powerfully to our
impression of the heroism and pathos of history, the
struggles and sufferings of humanity.'

The first incident in this history shown to Adam is the
murder of Abel. He is terrified by his first sight of death,
and asks

> is this the way
> I must return to native dust?   [xi. 462–3

Michael replies that there are many ways to death, and
presents the dreadful 'Lazar house' of diseases that will
afflict mankind. By these sights he is brought to realize the
suffering and degradation he has entailed on posterity.

Next he is shown the transition from pastoral to civilized
life; the growth of arts and learning, with their accompany-
ing luxury and vice; the growth of cities,

> Towns, and rural works between,
> Cities of men with lofty Gates and Towrs,
> [xi. 639–40

the establishment of armies, and the slaughter and devasta-
tion of wars. At this point Milton puts into Michael's
mouth one of his most powerful condemnations of the false
idea of the soldier as hero:

> For in those dayes Might onely shall be admir'd,
> And Valour and Heroic Vertue calld;
> To overcome in Battel, and subdue
> Nations, and bring home spoils with infinite
> Man-slaughter, shall be held the highest pitch
> Of human Glorie, and for Glorie done
> Of triumph, to be styl'd great Conquerors,
> Patrons of Mankind, Gods and Sons of Gods,
> Destroyers rightlier calld and Plagues of men.

[197]

Thus Fame shall be achiev'd, renown on Earth,
And what most merits fame in silence hid.

[xi. 689–99

Soon peace returns once more:

The brazen Throat of Warr had ceas't to roar,
All now was turnd to jollitie and game,
To luxurie and riot, feast and dance,
Marrying or prostituting, as befell,
Rape or Adulterie, where passing faire
Allur'd them; thence from Cups to civil Broils.

[xi. 713–8

Adam's comment on these alternating scenes of peace and war is,

for now I see
Peace to corrupt no less than Warr to waste.

[xi. 783–4

Amid these shifting scenes of strife and corruption is introduced Milton's typical hero, 'the one just man', who

spake much of Right and Wrong,
Of Justice, of Religion, Truth and Peace,
And Judgement from above.   [xi. 666–8

He is mocked, and silenced by violence. Then Noah appears and warns the godless world of its imminent doom,

But all in vain: which when he saw, he ceas'd
Contending, and remov'd his Tents farr off.

[xi. 726–7

The description of the Flood is one of the set-pieces of the poem, owing much to the description in Ovid's *Metamorphoses* but raised far above Ovid's wittiness by a stronger imagination:

the floating Vessel swum
Uplifted; and secure with beaked prow
Rode tilting ore the Waves, all dwellings else

Flood overwhelmd, and them with all thir pomp
Deep under water rould; Sea coverd Sea,
Sea without shore; and in thir Palaces
Where luxurie late reignd, Sea-monsters whelpd
And stabl'd.   [xi. 745–52

One remembers the lines in *Lycidas*:

Where thou perhaps under the whelming tide
Visitst the bottom of the monstrous world.

There is also the powerful description of the lost hill of
Paradise being swept by the flood down the Euphrates to
the Persian Gulf:

                        pusht by the horned flood,
With all his verdure spoilt and Trees adrift
Down the great River to the op'ning Gulf,
And there take root an Iland salt and bare,
The haunt of Seals and Orcs, and Sea-mews clang.
                                    [xi. 831–5

Is there a more telling vision of ruin and desolation, and all
that the Fall means to the Christian mind?

The only criticism one has of this long passage on the
Flood is that occasionally the poet, no doubt under Ovid's
influence, is a little too wordy; at lines 787–829 for instance
Adam is allowed to review all that he has been shown and to
moralize on it, even to describe the Flood all over again.
Milton fell into this fault because there is no press of action,
nothing to restrain him from the superfluity and iteration
of the preacher.

Book XI ends with the sight of the first rainbow in the
sky:

A dewie Cloud, and in the Cloud a Bow
Conspicuous with three listed colours gay,
Betok'ning peace from God, and Cov'nant new.
Whereat the heart of *Adam* erst so sad
Greatly rejoic'd, . . .   [ix. 865–9

[199]

Here is a natural climax and pause,

> Betwixt the world destroyd and world restor'd.
>
> [xii. 3

It is now that the method changes from vision to narration. Michael tells of Nimrod, the first king and tyrant, the first destroyer of man's natural liberty,

> which alwayes with right Reason dwells
> Twinnd, and from her hath no dividual being.
>
> [xii. 84–5

Then of the building of the Tower of Babel and the confusion of tongues; of God's promise to Abraham and his seed, as God's chosen people; of Moses leading the Israelites out of Egypt to the Promised Land; of their Judges and Kings; of their tribulations in the Babylonian exile and their return to Jerusalem. This history of the Jews, with all its vicissitudes, its moments of triumph and glory, its defeats and backslidings, culminates in the coming of the Messiah, his dying to save the world, his resurrection and reascension into Heaven. Adam stands in wonder at this final revelation:

> more wonderful
> Than that which by creation first brought forth
> Light out of darkness! full of doubt I stand,
> Whether I should repent me now of sin
> By mee done and occasiond, or rejoice
> Much more, . . .
>
> [xii. 471–6

In answer to Adam's question as to what will become of the faithful few left alone once more among 'the faithless herd' after Christ's return to Heaven, Michael emphasizes that the righteous will continue to suffer persecution, and wrong will seem to prevail, even among those in authority in Christ's church:

> Truth shall retire
> Bestuck with slandrous darts, and works of Faith

Rarely be found: so shall the World goe on,
To good malignant, to bad men benign,
Under her own weight groaning, till the day
Appear of respiration to the just
And vengeance to the wicked, at return
Of him so lately promis'd to thy aid,
The Womans seed, obscurely then foretold,
Now amplier known thy Saviour and thy Lord,
Last in the Clouds from Heav'n to be reveal'd
In glory of the Father, to dissolve
Satan with his perverted World, then raise
From the conflagrant mass, purg'd and refin'd,
New Heav'ns, new Earth, Ages of endless date
Founded in righteousness and peace and love,
To bring forth fruits, Joy and eternal Bliss.

[xii. 535–51

This exultant prophecy is said to betray the pessimism of a disillusioned man. Tillyard wrote of these lines, 'The comfort is nominal, the fundamental pessimism unmistakable. Milton seeks to comfort himself in an imagined new order, but it is not by any such distant possibility that his wound can be healed. For from his youth on Milton had nursed the hope that mankind would improve out of its own resources. . . . His hopes, elated for a time by political events, were dashed far below their former lowest point, never to recover. Mankind would never in this world be any better; and Milton cannot be comforted.' These remarks seem to me, if I may say so, quite perverse. The 'imagined new order' in which Milton sought 'nominal comfort' is the Christian faith in a redeemed world; Tillyard implies that Milton did not really believe in that 'distant possibility', but there is no evidence for thinking that he did not and ample evidence for thinking that he did. Secondly, Milton never, even in his youth, held the atheistical view of the modern communist, 'that mankind would improve out of its own resources'; he held that godfearing resolute men would improve by God's grace. Certainly his young enthusiasm for the Puritan revolution was to end in disappointment, but this did not disillusion him because his fundamental faith was not political but religious. His real faith held firm, in the face of political disaster and personal blindness, to the end. His teaching, from *Lycidas* on, is that earthly success and triumph are valueless by themselves; that ultimate victory can only be in the individual steadfast soul, seeking and standing by the truth under God. It may anger the out-and-out humanist that Milton thinks that eminently virtuous souls of this sort are few and far between, and therefore likely to be solitary; but that is to be angry at the obvious. And it does not follow, as may seem, that Milton regards the rest of mankind as damned; his favourite epithet for man is indeed 'frail', but it is spoken in compassion and he believes that all who repent will be saved – it is only the hardhearted malignant he would condemn. That the world is evil is not only Christian doctrine but apparent to all, and it is not optimism but sentimentalism to deny it. True optimism consists in recognizing the fact whilst holding to one's faith in the ultimate victory of good. Under Michael's instruction Adam has learnt this lesson:

> Henceforth I learn, that to obey is best,
> And love with feare the onely God, . . .
> Merciful over all his works, with good
> Still overcoming evil, and by small
> Accomplishing great things, by things deemd weak
> Subverting worldly strong, and worldly wise
> By simple meek; that suffering for Truths sake
> Is fortitude to highest victorie,
> And to the faithful Death the Gate of Life;
> Taught this by his example whom I now
> Acknowledge my Redeemer ever blest.   [xii. 561–73

This is the fulfilment of Adam as the hero of the poem.
  They now descend the hill, and Adam runs to the sleeping

Eve, who in her second dream in the poem has seen and heard all that has been revealed to him: she too is fortified with knowledge.

> And thus with words not sad she him receiv'd . . .
> In mee is no delay; with thee to goe
> Is to stay here; without thee here to staye
> Is to go hence unwilling; thou to mee
> Art all things under Heav'n, all places thou,
> Who for my wilful crime art banisht hence.
>
> [xii. 609–19

They are lovers again; if not the 'happie paire' first met in Paradise, yet 'not sad', and more experienced and confident in their dependence on each other and on God. There is not the rapture of 'With thee conversing I forget all time' nor, on the other hand, of Eve returning with the fruit to Adam, 'For bliss as thou hast part to me is bliss'; but they have found 'the Paradise within', and are ready to face a harder world.

The cherubim now descend to expel them from Paradise:

> all in bright array
> The Cherubim descended; on the ground
> Gliding meteorous, as Ev'ning Mist
> Ris'n from a River ore the marish glides,
> And gathers ground fast at the Labourers heel
> Homeward returning . . . whereat
> In either hand the hastning Angel caught
> Our lingring Parents, and to th' Eastern Gate
> Led them direct, and down the Cliff as fast
> To the subjected Plain; then disappear'd.
> They looking back, all th' Eastern side beheld
> Of Paradise, so late thir happie seat,
> Wav'd over by that flaming Brand, the Gate
> With dreadful Faces throngd and fierie Arms:
> Som natural tears they dropd, but wip'd them soon;
> The World was all before them, where to choose

Thir place of rest, and Providence thir guide:
They hand in hand with wandring steps and slow,
Through *Eden* took thir solitarie way.   [xii. 627–49

This consummate ending, as Prince points out, would not
have its full significance and effect without the vision of
world history in the previous thousand lines: 'To see "our
first parents" setting out into the world is to see them consciously entering on the long and patient work of human
history, which we have had presented to us.' And again he
notes that, 'The brief image of the labourer returning home
after a day's work in the fields is a very simple allusion to the
contents of Books XI and XII: it looks back and it looks
forward, and in this context of "dreadful Faces" and "fierie
Arms" it is especially effective, a moving invocation of the
life of toil and poverty and weariness, and also of homely
satisfactions – all the common experience of humanity –
which Adam and Eve must now undertake.' I would only
add that to me the strongest note there is of mutual affection
and trust, symbolized in that recurrent phrase, 'hand in
hand'.

These last two Books are seen then to justify themselves
poetically: in completing the central story of Adam and Eve
they complete the immense and noble structure of the poem.
And it can now be seen that this central story is less remote
from ordinary human interests than is usually thought and
said. It is true that Adam and Eve before the Fall are by
nature and situation different from any man and woman we
know, yet even in this paradisal state they are interesting for
their human characteristics and their human behaviour
under those special conditions. After the Fall they become
sinful mortals like ourselves and, although their characters
do not change, their change of state allows of their characters being more fully developed as ordinary human beings.
Then, at the close of the poem, they emerge clearly as individuals. Eliot on the contrary argues that, as our 'first

Parents', they never become ordinary individuals: 'These are not a man and woman such as any we know: if they were, they would not be Adam and Eve. They are the original Man and Woman, not types, but prototypes: if they were not set apart from ordinary humanity they would not be Adam and Eve. . . . They have ordinary humanity to the right degree, and yet are not, and should not be, ordinary mortals.' In so far as this is true it is true of the heroic characters in any epic; to fulfil their roles they are necessarily larger than life. Aeneas and Dido are representative rather than ordinary individuals in the same way as Adam and Eve; any difference in this respect is a question only of degree. As representatives of all mankind Adam and Eve might indeed be expected to be less individual and more remote from ordinary men and women than the heroes of other epics. This *a priori* expectation has been accepted by Eliot as fact. Yet that Adam and Eve do emerge as human individuals is attested by the impression made on us by the concluding lines of the poem.

In the course of the story we have grown familiar with them, but it is not perhaps until we watch them going down to our world of common experience that we realize how we have come to know and feel for them as fellow creatures; as they depart we recognize that they are nearer to us than those remote ancestors, our 'first Parents'. There is a poignancy in this farewell such as can only be felt for persons; one does not sympathize with types or prototypes. The individuality of Adam and Eve is surely a singular achievement with characters who at the same time represent the highest common factors in human nature; I can think of nothing in literature quite comparable to it. Appreciation of Milton's power of characterization is usually concentrated on Satan, but his success with Adam and Eve is a more difficult and rarer feat; so difficult and rare that readers do not credit it.

The importance of individualism in the characters of a

[205]

story is nowadays often exaggerated. The modern novel, dealing with the contemporary scene, has taught us to expect detailed studies of people and manners, until many have come to think that this is what matters most in a story. Yet it remains a rule of narrative art that the individualism of characters should not be developed beyond the needs of the story; characters are there to act out the story and its meaning, not just to be their idiosyncratic selves. Shakespeare, in the joy of creating such rich personalities as Falstaff and Shylock, allows them to run away with the plays, to break the intended patterns and confuse the issues. There was certainly no danger of this happening in *Paradise Lost*, nor was such a deliberate artist as Milton likely to commit the error. The scope for depicting individual characters and particular manners in *Paradise Lost* was as limited as it well could be, but within those limits Milton has fulfilled all the demands of his story, including the final one that the characters, in acting out the story and its meaning, should become persons we can know and care for. Here is another aspect of his art that calls for recognition.

INDEX

Addison, Joseph, (quoted) 24, 88–9; 90, 93; (quoted) 140, 190, 191

Africa, 107, 114, 196

Agricola, Georg, 76

Amboyna, 111

America, 107, 112

Amsterdam, 24, 25, 26

Anonymous biographer of Milton, 22; (quoted) 28, 29; 30, 31

Aquinas, Thomas, (quoted) 158

Arctic, 115, 116, 117

Aristotle, 52, 90

Arnold, Matthew, (quoted) 75; 91; (quoted) 94

Asia, 107, 196

Asia Minor, 105, 196

Aubrey, John, 22; (quoted) 26–30

Auden, W. H., (quoted) 14.

Augustine, 52

Baharim (Bahrein), 108

Bantam, 113

Barrow, Dr. Isaac, 26

Bayle, Pierre, 36

Beckford, William, 74

Bengal, 110, 113

Bentley, Richard, (quoted) 76; 90; (quoted) 110; 114, 115

Birch, Thomas, 36

Birds, Milton's descriptions of, 115, 122–3, 125

Birdwood, Sir George, (quoted) 114

Blake, William, 54

Boileau, Nicholas, 85–9

Brazil, 108

Bridges, Robert, 62

Browne, Sir Thomas, (quoted) 75

Burke, Edmund, 142

Byron, 43; the Byronic hero, 54

Cambridge, 26, 36

Camoens, Luis Vaz de, 109

Cape of Good Hope, 109, 111, 113

Carew, Thomas, 56

Cavaliers, 20

Chamber's Cyclopaedia, 112

Charles I, 23, 31, 74

Charles II, 39

Chaucer, Geoffrey, 72

China (Cathay), 115, 196

Clamor Regii Sanguinis, 32

Coleridge, S. T., 86; (quoted) 91, 92, 93; 114

Columbus, Christopher, 107

Connington-Nettleship edition of Virgil, (quoted) 70

Coromandel coast, 111

Cowper, William, (quoted) 36

Crashaw, Richard, (quoted) 70

Cromwell, Oliver, 23, 29, 31, 38

Daniel, Samuel, 73

Dante, Alighieri, 40, 42, 45, 101, 119, 120, 123, 177

Darbishire, Helen, 23, 28, 35; (quoted) 74, 141, 142, 185–6, 187

Davenant, Sir William, 28

Donne, John, 56, 63

Drake, Sir Francis, 111

Drayton, Michael, 73

Dryden, John, 23, 29, 30, 62; (quoted) 87, 111

Dutch, 111, 112, 114

East India Company, 111

East Indies, 107, 111, 112, 115

East, Near and Far, 107, 108, 112

Edward VI's Second Prayer Book, (quoted) 60

Egypt, 105, 107

Eliot, T. S., (quoted) 14, 63, 64, 65;
    66; (quoted) 75, 79; 83; (quoted)
    84; 121; (quoted) 124-5, 192,
    196, 204-5, 205
Elzevir, Daniel, 24
Equator, 113
Equinoctial winds, 113
Ethiopian Sea, 110
Euphrates, 199

Fenton, Elijah, 35, 36
Fitch, Ralph, 108
Foresthill, 27
Foster, William, 108 (f'note)
France, 29, 112, 113
French Academy, the, 85

Ganges, 111, 113
Gardner, Helen, 54
Greece, 105
Greeks, 107
Greek tragedy, 42
Greenwich, 116
Grierson, Sir Herbert, (quoted)
    18, 19, 157
Guinea, 113

Hakluyt, Richard, 108 (f'note);
    (quoted) 108; 109, 111, 112, 113,
    115; (quoted) 116-17
Hanford, James Holly, 56, (quoted)
    94
Hardy, Thomas, 42, 43
Hazlitt, William, (quoted) 68, 80,
    123
Herrick, Robert, 56
Hobbes, Thomas, (quoted) 87
Holland, 25, 112
Homer, 42, 55, 65, 85, 86, 88, 89,
    90, 95; (quoted) 100; 103, 128
Hooker, Richard, 49
Hopkins, Gerard Manley, 39
Housman, A. E., 62

Ind, India, 107, 108, 109, 196

Indian Ocean, 111

James, Henry, 45, 192
Jebb, R. C., (quoted) 95
Jenkins, Sir Leoline, 25
Johnson, Samuel, (quoted) 30; 31,
    35; (quoted) 36, 37, 38, 39; 40,
    44; (quoted) 64, 135, 140
Jonson, Ben, 64
Joyce, James, 65; (quoted) 106

Keats, John, 43
Ker, W. P., (quoted) 85; 94;
    (quoted) 109

Landor, Walter Savage, (quoted) 80,
    84, 150, 186
Lawlor, J. J., (quoted) 51
Lewis, C. S., (quoted) 104, 106,
    158, 191
Locke, J. Courtenay, 108 (f'note)
Longinus, 86, 90
Louis XIV, 112
Lucretius, 42
Lyttleton's *Latin-English Dictionary*,
    112

Malacca, 108
Malay Archipelago, 111
Malone, Edmund, (quoted) 35; 36
Marlowe, Christopher, 54; (quoted)
    153
Marvell, Andrew, 29
Masson, David, 24, 40; (quoted)
    93-4
Mesopotamia, 108
Mexico, 108
Milton, Anne, (Milton's eldest
    daughter), 28
Milton, Deborah (Milton's youngest
    daughter), 27, 33, 34
Milton, Elizabeth, *née* Minshull
    (Milton's third wife), 19

Milton, John. Writings, other than *Paradise Lost*, referred to or quoted: *Areopagitica*, (quoted) 117; *Commonplace Book*, 58; *Comus*, 68, 70; (quoted) 105, 159; *De Doctrina Christiana*, 24, 26, 42, 46; (quoted) 47, 48, 49, 50, 141, 179; *Doctrine and Discipline of Divorce*, 32, 37, 40; (quoted) 58, 59, 156; Eikonoklastes, 23; (quoted) 74; *Il Penseroso*, 70; *Italian Sonnets*, 56; *Latin Elegies*, (quoted) 56; *Letters of State*, 22, 24; *Lycidas*, 123; (quoted) 199; 202; *Nativity Ode*, (quoted) 105; *Of Education*, (quoted) 117; *Paradise Regain'd*, 55, 70, 131, 182, 195; *Pro Populo Anglicano Defensio*, 23, 55; *Samson Agonistes*, 18, 19, 20, 55, 131, 191; *Tetrachordon*, (quoted) 60

Milton, Katharine, *née* Woodcock (Milton's second wife), 19, 38

Milton, Mary (Milton's first wife). See under Powell.

Milton, Mary (Milton's second daughter), 33

Modern Language Review, 37 (f'note), 40

Moluccas, 196

Moscow, 116

Newman, John Henry, (quoted) 32

Newton, Thomas, 35, 36

Nimeguen, English embassy at, 25

North-east and north-west passages, 115–17

Oxford English Dictionary, 72, 74

Ormuz, 108–9

Ovid, (quoted) 57; 58, 198, 199

Pagett, Dr. Nathan, 30

Parker, R. W., 38

Pattison, Mark, 191

Paul, St., (quoted) 59; 157, 158

Pearce, Zachary, (quoted) 90; 92

Pepys, Samuel, 24, 25

Perrault, Charles, 85, 88, 89

Persia, 108

Persian Gulf, 108, 199

Petrarch, 56

Petsora, 116

Pettus, Sir John, 77

Phillips, Edward, (quoted) 20–1; 22, 24; (quoted) 27–8; 36, 37, 40

Phillips, John, 26–7

Pindar, 86

Pope, Alexander, 45; (quoted) 46, 81, 90; 123

Portugal, 112

Portuguese, 111, 112, 114

Powell, Mary, 19, 20, 21, 27, 32, 37, 38, 58

Powell family, 27, 28

Prince, F. T., (quoted) 192; 193; (quoted) 196–7, 204

Proctor, Sherwin, (quoted) 94

Purchas, Samuel, (quoted) 107–8; 108 (f'note); (quoted) 108–9; 109; (quoted) 111; 112; (quoted) 113; 114, 115

Puritans, 20, 52

Quarrel of the Ancients and Moderns, 85–6

Raleigh, Professor Walter, (quoted) 94

Restoration, the, 8, 33; Restoration London, 16

Richardson, Jonathan, (quoted) 17; 22, 28; (quoted) 32–5; 36; (quoted) 71

Robinson, Henry Crabb, 91

Roche, Giles de la, 112–13

Rome, 105, 196

Roman Church, 123

Rotterdam, 25

Roundheads, 20

Ruskin, John, (quoted) 101, 103
Russell, Mr., of St. Bride's church-yard, Milton's tailor and landlord, 27
Russia, 116, 117

St. Martin's Le Grand Lane, 27
Salmasius, 19, 20, 32, 55
Sandys, George, 65
Schlegel, Friedrich von, (quoted) 92
Shakespeare, William, 20, 54; (quoted) 62; 63; (quoted) 69, 70, 71, 72, 73; 75, 77, 206
Shawcross, J., (quoted) 92
Shelley, P. B., 43, 54
Sir Orfeo, 105
Skinner, Daniel, 26
Skinner, Daniel, Jr., 24–8, 30
Smart, J. S., 56
Southern hemisphere, 114
South Pole, 114
Spain, 112
Spanish, 112
Spenser, Edmund, his grandson, 28; *The Faerie Queene*, 68, 156
Spice Islands, 111.
'Spicie Drugs', 111–12
State Paper Office, Whitehall, 26
Stein, Alfred, 131
Suckling, Sir John, 56
Swift, Jonathan, 123
Sylvester, Joshua, 153

Taylor, Jeremy, (quoted) 72
Teneriffe, 112
Tennyson, Alfred, (quoted) 110
Ternate, 110, 111
Thomas, Edward, 108 (f'note)
Tidore, 110, 111

Tillotson, Geoffrey, (quoted) 69
Tillyard, E. M. W., 17; (quoted) 100, 138–9; 151; (quoted) 160; 161; (quoted) 176, 201
Times Literary Supplement, (quoted) 21
Toland, John, 22, 36, 40
Tonson, Jacob, (quoted) 28–9
Trade, 108, 109, 110, 111, 112
Trade winds, 110, 113
Trading flood, 110
Trinity College, Cambridge, 24, 26

Vasco da Gama, 109
Verity, A. W., (quoted) 18; 19; (quoted) 21, 98, 115, 124–5, 131
Villon, Annette, 21
Virgil, 42, 55, 65; (quoted) 70; 88, 89, 90, 103, 140, 178, 191–2, 205

Waldock, A. J. A., 45; (quoted) 154–5, 163, 164; 165; (quoted) 175, 176–7; 178
Warton, Thomas, (quoted) 24, 30
Webbe, William, 73
Wellington, Duke of, 22
West Indies, 107
Wheeler, James, 94 (f'note)
Williams, Charles, 53, 54
Williamson, Sir Joseph, 24–6
Willoughby, Sir Hugh, 116–17
Winstanley, William, (quoted) 23
Wood, Anthony, (quoted) 22; 28; (quoted) 30, 31, 32; 36
Wordsworth, William, 21; (quoted) 35; 43; 63; (quoted) 75; 83, 91, 92; (quoted) 92–3, 161; 191
Wright, Dr., 'an aged clergyman in Dorsetshire', 17
Wycliffe, John, 72